More Praise for *Unusually Excellent*

"There are many parallels between coaching a professional sports team and leading a business or civic organization. John hits the bulls eye of what is crucial to leading and winning in a high performance team environment. He lays out a model that any leader can put into action in a powerful way. This book will challenge your commitment to the disciplines that really work; but if you choose to follow these ideas, you'll be rewarded. *Unusually Excellent* belongs in every leader's office with the pages well worn from repeated readings."

—Steve Mariucci, former head coach, San Francisco 49ers,
Detroit Lions; analyst, NFL Network

"*Unusually Excellent* will call you to higher ground as a leader and give you the insights, context, and tools to get there. John Hamm's clear, sage advice and stark authenticity will inform your leadership decisions, large and small. And he reminds you, sometimes with a dose of tough love, of who you are at your core, and explains why some of what you do works and some doesn't. This book is a gift to my growth as a leader, and my new leadership reference manual."

—Ted Mitchell, CEO, The NewSchools Venture Fund;
president, California State Board of Education

"Finally! A compelling, cogent, back-to-basics book for leaders navigating the complex terrain of a global, interconnected, 24/7 world. In *Unusually Excellent*, John Hamm is an expert coach for leaders, prodding us to skip the latest fads and instead take a fresh look at the power of fundamentals, the necessary and timeless essentials of character, competence and consequence. There are dozens of immediately usable insights here—something for everyone. This book should be on every leader's bookshelf."

—Linda Rottenberg, co-founder and CEO, Endeavor.Org

"I just love *Unusually Excellent*. It's classic Hamm—insightful, compelling, and actionable. I only wish I had read this when I was starting Military.com. It's impossible to read this book and not find lots of new and powerful ideas for leading your organization. I plan to give a copy to all the CEOs I know."

—Chris Michel, CEO and founder,
Military.Com and Affinity Labs (Monster); founder, Nautilus Ventures

"*Unusually Excellent* is simply an unusually excellent read. It just might be the missing piece of the leadership puzzle for you as a manager at any level of your organization. John brings together the nine essentials of leadership to show you that it's not about who you are, but rather how you think and what you do. It will help you understand what leadership really means and energize your passion for leading."

—Michael Fitzpatrick, general partner,
Seabury Ventures; former CEO, E-Tek Dynamics;
former president and CEO Pacific Telesis

"This is a significant contribution to the field. This framework of effective leadership is energizing, prescriptive, and provides a holistic view which is a must read for young as well as experienced leaders in an ever more complex world of business."

—Stefan Sjöström, General Manager,
Public Sector, Microsoft Western Europe

UNUSUALLY EXCELLENT

The Necessary Nine Skills Required for the Practice of Great Leadership

John Hamm

JOSSEY-BASS
A Wiley Imprint
www.josseybass.com

Published by Jossey-Bass
A Wiley Imprint
989 Market Street, San Francisco, CA 94103-1741—www.josseybass.com

Jossey-Bass books and products are available through most bookstores. To contact Jossey-Bass directly call our Customer Care Department within the U.S. at 800-956-7739, outside the U.S. at 317-572-3986, or fax 317-572-4002.

Jossey-Bass also publishes its books in a variety of electronic formats. Some content that appears in print may not be available in electronic books.

Library of Congress Cataloging-in-Publication Data
Hamm, John, 1959–
  Unusually excellent : the necessary nine skills required for the practice of great leadership / John Hamm.
    p. cm.
  Includes index.
  ISBN 978-0-470-92843-1
  1. Leadership.   2. Values.   I. Title.
  HD57.7.H3455 2011
  658.4'092—dc22

                                                                            2010045595

Printed in the United States of America

FIRST EDITION

HB Printing   10 9 8 7 6 5 4 3

● CONTENTS

To Joanna—

An Unusually Excellent wife and partner—
She lives the values of excellence

To our children—

Andie, Perry, Arthur, and Taylor—
They remind us of the important things in life

● FOREWORD

By GEOFFREY MOORE

R eal leadership in daily practice is far from the commonly understood caricature of leadership. We *don't* really know what leadership means, in part because it never means quite the same thing
twice. It does *not* always stand for great things by definition. Indeed,
much of the time its most powerful acts pass unnoticed, even when
we are looking for them. And although it is always demonstrated by
our words and actions, those are so dependent on who we are at the
time that they *cannot* be learned by example or by rule.

Emerson has a great line: "God *is*, not *was*." The same is true of
leadership. It is the performance in the moment, not the performance in the mind, that matters. Yes, there is preparation, and
indeed, the more you prepare, the better your chances. But there is
no script, or rather there are a myriad of scripts all potentially about
to unfold, and you have to choose one, when you yourself are far
from sure but, ideally, unwavering. And you must live with the
inevitable fallibility of some of those choices, even as you can take
pride in the successes of others.

To lead well, as this book makes deeply and powerfully clear, is
first and foremost to know yourself, and second to put yourself in

service to whatever you value most deeply. If you adopt that posture, whatever follows can be incorporated into making yourself a better leader. And it is the purpose of this book to help you do so.

There is a model provided herein—and, similar in nature to the framework I put forth in *Crossing the Chasm*, this structure allows you to locate yourself on the leadership playing field. Once you know where you are, you will see much more clearly your choices for action. In our strategy practice at TCG Advisors with clients worldwide, we frequently see the opportunity for leaders to use tools like this to support their work.

Like a good golf instructor (which he is, by the way), John Hamm teaches by situation, by principle, and by illustration, all in one. The stories he tells, the lessons he relates, the way he takes you through the details of a performance, the way he helps you think about it once it is over and done—it is all in service to showing you what good leadership looks and feels like, and what bad leadership looks and feels like. But as with coaching in any sport, it comes down to you taking personal ownership of the outcome: you taking the risk and responsibility of action, and you owning both your successes and your shortfalls.

You can treat this book as an easy read, for it is that, but that would be a waste. Treat it instead as a call to a great adventure— your adventure—and use John as a trusted guide. Work with him to develop yourself into a powerful leader in service to something deeply worthwhile. There is no higher calling, nor anything that the world needs more in our time.

Geoffrey Moore
September 2010

● INTRODUCTION

As a leadership teacher and consultant—and as a scratch golfer—one of my most interesting—and favorite—clients is TaylorMade-adidas Golf, the world's leading manufacturer of performance golf equipment.

If you play golf, or at least follow the PGA Tour, you have probably heard of TaylorMade's Performance Center in Carlsbad, California—it's known as "The Kingdom."

Each winter, many of the world's finest professional golfers visit The Kingdom, usually with their coaches in tow, ostensibly to get precisely fitted for professional-grade metal-woods, irons, wedges, and putters. And The Kingdom offers the latest, state-of-the-art equipment—high-speed digital cameras, launch monitors, lasers, and computers—to do just that. For that task, it is the best (and certainly the most beautiful) such facility on Earth.

But there is another story to The Kingdom—one that I learned only with insider access to watch and study these PGA and LPGA pros and their coaches in action. And what I learned there is the revelation that led to the writing of this book.

You see, these golfers are the very best in their field—professional, play-for-money, dog-eat-dog competitive golf. They are the sports equivalent of Fortune 500 CEOs. The best in their business. And

often, when they arrive at The Kingdom, they are frustrated or per-
plexed with their recent performance. Something has gone wrong
with their game, and it is showing up in their scores. This problem
may represent only one or two strokes per round—but at the world-
class level at which these athletes play this game, that can be the
difference between victory and finishing out of the money. A year
or two of these kinds of problems and they will lose their playing
privileges on the professional Tour and their livelihood will have
disappeared.

Inevitably, these players have their own ideas about what they
are doing wrong when they arrive—and just as inevitably, those
theories are misplaced.

Now, you might imagine (as I initially did) that the first thing
these Tour pros and their coaches would do is to head into the lab,
hook up to the test equipment, and begin measuring every detail of
that golfer's swing and ball flight. But you would be wrong. In fact,
what typically happens is just the opposite—and is the lowest-tech
first step imaginable: golfer and coach begin by heading out to the
range to hit some practice balls.

The first time I saw this I was so astonished that I found an
excuse to hang around the range as well, hoping to eavesdrop on
this fascinating coaching conversation. And what I heard was truly
eye-opening.

What I had expected was that coach and golfer would focus
on the problem at hand, analyzing and then correcting, on the spot,
the errors the player believed were responsible. Instead, even when
the player wanted to address "the problem" as he or she imagined
it, invariably the coach politely and deceptively ignored that line
of thought and instead insisted that the golfer begin with the most
basic fundamentals of grip, stance, posture, ball position, and aim.
I had expected to hear pearls of great wisdom; what I heard instead
was the same kind of elementary instruction taking place at that
moment on municipal golf courses around the country.

What was going on here? These were some of the greatest
golfers on the planet, being taught by the most celebrated swing

coaches alive. Why were they focusing on fundamentals that these champion golfers must have first heard when they were nine years old? Why, if the golfer thought he or she needed a slight change to their equipment, didn't they just head into the test center and have something fabricated?

But the more I listened, the more I understood what was really going on. I began to appreciate that no matter how talented and successful the golfer, and no matter how strong their opinion about what had gone wrong, most were in fact ill-suited to diagnose their own performance. Why? Human nature. Even the best performers, in any field, will slowly—and imperceptibly—stray away from the fundamentals of their craft. This drift is almost always invisible to them. The human nature part is that losing precision in the fundamentals is exactly the *last* thing most accomplished people would imagine or will accept as the cause. Instead, left to their own devices, they look elsewhere—mostly to much more complex theories of the cause—and pursue fixes that often do more harm than good. They can't imagine that the cause of the current breakdown could be something so simple, and right in front of them. They can't imagine that they couldn't see it if it were.

Great coaches understand this. They know that the path to a solution often starts with a revisit to those fundamentals—and only then can the confusion be untangled and the problem is properly identified, isolated, and attacked. I can't tell you how many times I've watched these professional golfers, after an hour of a supervised, disciplined return to the basics, begin to hit the ball as well as they ever have, and predictably turn to their coach and say, "That was it. You're a genius."

Sometimes that solution is as simple as where the ball is placed in relation to the player's feet—an inch or less change that the player, too close to the problem, couldn't see. Sometimes it actually is the length, weight, or lie angle of the club—and then, and only then, the golfer and coach finally enter The Kingdom for some equipment tweaks by the equipment gurus.

As I watched this small miracle occur again and again, it struck me that I was seeing a universal truth—one that could be readily applied to the world of business management and leadership. For thirty years now, we have been inundated with endless new fads and theories about how to be a good leader. In the process, most of us have been exposed numerous times—if only under different names and in piecemeal—to all of the essential truths about leadership.

But, like those world-class golfers, even the best leaders can and do stray from those fundamentals over time—and then regularly misdiagnose the cause of the problems. They need some outside help—a fresh set of eyes—but few know it. And, like athletes, organizational leaders often struggle to see or admit their own failures. They subconsciously believe they can't reveal a weakness in their game, or that the costs to their career and their companies are too great. From there, fear sets in, they turn up the heat on themselves, and they are not inclined to look to coaches or other mentors. Instead, they push on, redoubling their efforts, denying or ignoring the results—and, like those golfers, risk amplifying their errors rather than resolving them. Like the golfer's challenge, these mistakes often occur as a small group of related errors, and then there's a domino effect: one thing leads to another, and this set of issues conspires to confound and confuse the player. It is not obvious how to untangle this new strain of problem born of several fundamentals that are out of tune. At this point, self-diagnosis is a disaster waiting to happen. To paraphrase Albert Einstein's famous quote, we can't solve a problem using the same thinking that created it. Tragically, some leaders, like some golfers, never escape their own thinking and thus don't seek outside support in the midst of this kind of complex, self-generated mess. They are then blindly trapped in a maddening, sometimes desperate effort to find the game they once knew they had.

There is a reason that Ben Hogan's *Five Lessons: The Modern Fundamentals of Golf* remains a perennial best seller more than five decades after it was written. It is the book that serious golfers regularly revisit to walk and rewalk them through the fundamentals of their sport—the fundamentals that the finest ball striker in the history of the game knew were the essentials to great results.

I've written *Unusually Excellent* to be that book for business and organizational leadership. I know, from my coaching practice with leaders at all levels, that professional managers in all fields— whether they are just starting out, in the middle of their careers, or facing the legacy they will leave behind—need to revisit the fundamentals of their own leadership practices regularly and systematically, just as athletes do. I've written this book to be the expert coach at their side, watching them work, realigning them back to their center—which made them successful in the past, but from which they have inevitably and insidiously strayed. At this level, there are no tricks, no fads, no conceits, only the enduring touchstones of great leadership.

It is only by returning to these essentials, and newly committing to them again, that we can travel that "last mile" from being good leaders to becoming great ones. The path to that kind of greatness, to becoming an unusually excellent leader, begins right here in the pages that follow—in the Nine Essentials of leadership that can become your private coach. A coach who is always available to remind you and walk you through the fundamentals.

The Five W's (and One H) of Leadership

This is a book *for* leaders, not about them. It is about the *practice* of leadership over the course of a long career, not the theory of leadership learned over a weekend. It is not about the introduction of clever new notions of leadership, but about the *reassertion* of proven precepts. Finally, it is not an introduction to leadership, but an operating manual for all of those who are already engaged as leaders, at any level, whether at the beginning, middle, or end of their careers.

This book is the product of a quarter-century of work as a leader in companies of various sizes, from start-ups to Fortune 100 firms; and over a decade as an investor and board member evaluating and supporting leaders, as a leadership coach to CEOs, and finally as a university professor specializing in the study of leadership. During this time, I have worked in depth with more than a hundred senior leaders, most of them CEOs, and have spent more than ten thousand hours in practice on the subject of organizational leadership.

What all this experience has taught me—and what I hope imbues every page of this book—is that real practitioners of great leadership are successful by mastering a *very specific set of essential rules and practices* and behaving according to those fundamentals day after day in whatever way the environment or circumstances demand. None of these principles are new—on the contrary, they may be as old as leadership itself—but they are regularly forgotten. And even when they are remembered, they must be constantly tested and updated or they lose their power.

To excel as a leader, you not only must know what these essentials look like, but you must also understand

- *How* those essentials combine logically in an overall model of leadership
- *Why* those essentials are so important—and have always been important—in the making of great leaders
- *What* are the underlying principles of human nature and human interaction they direct and amplify
- *When* these essentials are to be applied, both situation-specific and over the course of a professional career
- *Who* are the subjects of these essentials—that is, the people being led—and how their needs are best met and their performance maximized
- *Where* these essentials are best applied to achieve the maximum impact upon productivity, morale, force multiplication, profit—and, ultimately, reputation

The unfolding of these core principles—there are nine of them—and how they relate to one another form the heart of this

book. Though often forgotten or lost in the noise, these core principles, these essentials, never change. Indeed, we can find their echoes
in the stories of "unusually excellent" leaders, real and fictional,
throughout history—from Odysseus to Henry V to Eisenhower—but
they must be regularly rewritten to reflect the changes in context
brought by culture, technology, and competition.

My goal in this book is not to teach you these essential skills per
se, but to *remind* you of them. I say "remind" because the odds are
very high that you've heard all of them before—but they were buried
in the latest leadership or management fad program, or given insufficient attention compared to some other popular "truth"—or worst
of all, declared obsolete, or at least anachronistic, in the modern
world.

They are nothing of the sort. Rather, they are core human
truths tested, refined, and purified in the fires and crucibles of war,
empire, survival, and athletic competition. Not only are these principles not obsolete, they may in fact *never* be obsolete—not as long
as we are human beings being led by other human beings. Rather,
the real question, the puzzle for each of us to solve, is this: *How do
we apply these essentials to the unique leadership situation in which we
find ourselves?*

I'm going to present these nine essential leadership skills—
cogently, memorably, and, for the first time, all in one place, in logical harmony with each other. And I'm going to attack each of those
lessons from different directions: case studies, psychology, anecdotes
and stories, empirical evidence and logical analysis—in the belief
that one or more of these will resonate with you and embed this content permanently into the way you manage your career. Finally, I'm
going to put these nine diverse rules into their larger context by providing a logical, and unforgettable, taxonomy of leadership—so that
you not only understand each of these essentials, but understand
how they interact with each other to produce a complete model of
applied leadership over the course of a full career.

Can I guarantee that, at this point in your career, you will fully
understand or appreciate every concept presented in the pages to

come? No. However, I'm reminded of the old adage—"We don't see things as they are, but rather as we are." You will read this book from where you are in your life as a leader—right now. And you can read it again a year or five years from now, or the night before an important all-hands or offsite meeting with your team—and allow yourself the opportunity to tune-up all the things you know but just needed a friendly reminder of to sharpen your memory in ways that enable your best work. Becoming aware of the subtle difference between you at your best and you at your normal is sometimes exactly what the situation calls for, and can make the difference between something ordinary and something extraordinary.

That said, even the young junior manager in his or her first leadership job will come away from this book having at least been exposed to all of the nine essentials of leadership, positioned in a framework that will resonate with their logical understanding and experience of the world—and will have them in hand when needed. As for the veteran manager, many of the lessons in this book will be a reinforcement of what he or she already knows, perhaps articulated in a powerful new way not seen before. For the veteran, however, the final section of the book will address topics— reputation, legacy, and consequences—that are rarely even spoken of, much less put into the pages of a book. These are the quiet con- versations that, until now, successful men and women typically have only with themselves, a trusted mentor, or a spouse. I've decided to take them head-on. And because many veteran leaders only discover—to their dismay—that building a reputation starts at the beginning of a career, not at its end, this book serves as a timely heads-up to young leaders as well.

Leaders Lead

Besides a tendency to ignore the proven lessons of the past, fad leadership theories also usually treat leadership as a kind of tool kit, a grab-bag of predetermined moves that magically appear at the right moment to fit the right problem and can be executed mechanistically.

Nothing could be further from the truth. As I'm going to show you, true leadership is an organic process, as much the product of character as of technique. It doesn't exist in discrete moments, but is made manifest over the course of a career of leading people. And it isn't a single concept, but a phenomenological *field*—that is, it is composed of actions, ideas, emotions, cultural forces, history, and expectations that exist together in a system. Yes, understanding leadership is a systems understanding—nothing happens in a silo.

You also can't just pull out "leadership technique number four" and swing it at a random problem. For one thing, the theoretical solution is almost always a poor fit to the messy real-life problem you face. Moreover, *leaders lead*: you can't just pick up a tool and expect it to work on its own; *you have to learn how to apply it*. To assume that an ambitious manager can attend a seminar on employee motivation and then go back and effectively implement those ideas, is like handing a 4-iron to someone who has never played golf but has watched it on TV, and expecting him or her to hit the ball cleanly through an opening in the trees back to the fairway.

Finally, management challenges, crises—and even opportunities—are not distinct events. There is rarely a precise moment when one can be said to begin; and they are rarely ever fully solved. Instead, they often emerge (as you only discover later) slowly and surreptitiously—until they suddenly burst on the scene, demanding a solution. By the same token, their resolution is almost always incomplete—and what remains unsolved sows the seeds of the next set of challenges, crises, and opportunities.

My belief, confirmed over decades of working with some of the world's top business leaders, is that leadership is enduring, dynamic, and simple in theory but complex in execution; that it is a lifelong or career-long journey of mastery; and that, like other deeply personal commitments of service, there is no particular destination, no end zone or finish line. It is the learning—and the satisfaction in knowing that you are more skilled and effective this year than you were last, and so on, looking forward—that keeps this a game worth playing, and makes the time you'll spend leading a worthy and noble use of your time and energy, and worth the opportunity cost of the alternatives in front of you.

It is in recognition of this continuum that I tend to stay away from using the notion of nine "rules" of leadership and instead use terms like "essentials" and "principles"—because this time-tested wisdom only serves as the ground on which a host of other factors must be deployed to construct short-term solutions and long-term strategies. Put another way, the Nine Essentials of this book are only a framework—albeit a tested and effective one—on which to hang all of the other situational and timely factors that constitute great leadership. These principles are the base from which leaders can tap all of their other faculties, experiences, intuition, and resources to help the organization move forward at the maximum safe rate of speed. However, to get these wrong, or to not honor their place in the solution, is to fall for the temptation of what simply won't work.

The Three Games of Leadership

As you're already discovering—mainly because I tend to use athletic metaphors—I am a huge sports fan and student of athletic excellence. And as the TaylorMade story suggests, as much as I admire great athletes and what they can do, I'm equally impressed by the best coaches and managers.

Just as sports—with its clearly defined rules, competition, heroics, and winners and losers—is a proxy for the larger world, coaching is a specific instance of leadership. Years of preparation, of recruiting, team-building, and training, can go out the window with a handful of poorly planned or poorly executed plays; and the most carefully crafted strategy can be voided by an injury just moments after the game begins.

Great coaches have an astounding skill for dealing with wide spectra of time and experience. When they are building the team, their perspective can extend years into the future. Yet during a game their decisions are made in real time and the impact is measured in minutes or seconds. Similarly, they go many months on a very predictable schedule running workouts and holding meetings—only to find themselves in the chaos of a game, enduring the most unpredictable and stressful work imaginable. And, let us not forget, they constantly live with the knowledge that, though the odds are against their ever being victorious, their customers (fans) expect them to win every game, and they are haunted by the realization that one mistake could end their careers and fortunes.

Coaches and managers are thus continuously tested in the crucible of leadership. As such, to survive, they need to maintain, literally, the ultimate "view of the field." This expanded view enables them to parse, plan, and prioritize their time, their energy, and their actions in preparation for each game, during the game, and in the game's aftermath.

This means that for them—and for you—there isn't just one, but *three* fields of play occurring simultaneously as you lead your organization. I believe it is absolutely essential that, as a leader, you are always mindful of these three distinct domains of leadership skills and appreciate that you continuously attend to each.

That's why there are three major sections of this book.

Part One, Credibility, is a matter of *character*. Leaders are at all times engaged in the process of establishing or earning, affirming or restoring, ruining or fixing, dismantling or cementing their *right to lead*—their leadership equity, their organizational loyalty.

Ultimately, this right can be exercised only if you have established your *credibility* with those you ask to follow you—and (if necessary) with those who confer on you the role of leader. On the one hand, although the *authority* to lead is a structural consequence of hierarchical or positional power granted legally or by decree, over time it is wholly inadequate to achieve the results to which most leaders aspire; the most talented people are never led by authority, and the best effort of the entire organization is at risk in a context of command and control. Credibility, on the other hand, is the sinew that binds teams to leaders, individually and collectively, and ultimately prepares both for the unavoidable tough times that will inevitably strain this relationship.

Credibility can be established by almost anyone for a short period of time. But it can be sustained only if those you lead genuinely *trust* you—and earning and maintaining that trust ultimately comes down to one thing: your character as a person and as a leader. In the end, as the ancients have taught us for millennia, character is destiny.

Part Two, Competence, is a matter of *skill*. Leaders are expected to be highly skilled regarding the tasks, processes, conversations, and judgments that create the intended results. The assets and techniques at the leader's disposal are people, strategies, and the management of execution. We expect our leaders to deploy these assets and use these tools skillfully—and in return we offer them our time and talents. And we hold our leaders accountable for their ability to create and increase the value of the enterprise—or at least that part of the organization they lead.

Credibility is the starting line, the "ante" into the game of leadership. However, as an example, we would never allow a doctor to treat us if we did not believe that he or she was, first and foremost, professionally competent, regardless of our affinity for him or her personally. Ultimately, and contrary to common wisdom, that competence trumps how authentic, trustworthy, or compelling we perceive that person to be. Leaders who are real winners attract followers with their credibility; they keep them on the team with their competence. It is only on the field, in the thick of the game, that we also begin to separate how we feel about a leader emotionally and how we experience that leader professionally. In other words, this is where we gain *respect* for a leader's skills, competencies, and ability to lead the processes and decisions that guide the organization's resources in executing today's operations and tomorrow's strategies. Popularity is nice; respect is essential.

Part Three, Consequences, is *the impact we have as leaders on the careers and lives of those we lead*. As followers, we are guided by the personal values of our leaders to gradually build an organizational culture—a system of behaviors and rewards aligned with *values*—that reflects and supports the deepest beliefs of the leader. A leader is always affecting his or her credibility in obvious and subtle ways; so too is that leader also constantly building their inescapable reputation through their actions. It is the outcomes and the subsequent stories of day-to-day real life in the organization that form our opinions and establish our regard for our leaders.

This organizational *culture*, its accumulation of legends, folklore, and prejudices, leads to *legacy*—those ideals and values by which we remember our leaders. A leader's legacy is larger than the leader, and in turn creates still more stories and folklore within the organization. Think of the impact of Jack Welch and David Packard as leaders, and how their legacy and the values they established continued to grow long after they passed the baton to their successors.

If leaders can lead in the moment, face-to face with the issues of the day, yet simultaneously hold a deep respect and appreciation for how their actions will be recorded, interpreted, and remembered after they are gone, they will have much more regard for the impact of their decisions, communications, and actions—especially those that have real *consequences* to the people around them.

The Necessary Nine

Credibility is a matter of character, and earns the right to lead. *Competence* is a matter of skill, and earns respect. And *consequence* is a matter of values, and earns reputation. These are the three overarching categories for the nine essentials of leadership. Within each category lie three essential precepts, each linked conceptually to the two others. Here is the full model, as it will be used in this book:

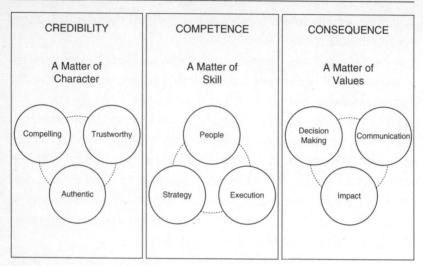

Figure I.1. Unusually Excellent: The Essential Skills

I'll bet that at some time in your education or your career you have seen every one of these essentials. But I'll also bet you've never seen them arrayed like this—nor realized how all of them interact to create a powerful synthesis that is greater than the sum of all of them.

It is this higher plane of leadership—the one that emerges from the virtuous cycle of all of these essentials *working together* in a consistent manner, over the course of a career—that creates what I've come to call—and have entitled this book—*Unusually Excellent* leadership.

These Unusually Excellent leaders are rare—perhaps one or two in a hundred. But that doesn't mean you can't be one of them. Talent and aptitude matter, of course. So do timing and opportunity. But I'm convinced that what keeps good leaders from becoming great ones is often just a matter of either not appreciating the need for *all* of these essentials to be in place, and showing up in their day-to-day leadership behaviors—or, more tragically, realizing it too late. To learn, we must realize and accept what we don't know and begin to seek that knowledge at that moment.

How many talented leaders have lost their credibility early in their careers and borne that stigma ever after? How many executives have proven themselves gifted at execution but not at strategy, and have pulled their organizations down for lack of a plan? And how many otherwise capable leaders have failed to get their organizations to follow because they failed to communicate well enough to enlist them?

You don't have to share that fate. You can be that one in a hundred, that unusually excellent leader. Look again at that chart of leadership essentials. They may be difficult, but they aren't complicated—and there are only nine of them. And I'm here to show you how to achieve each of them.

Every day you waste as a leader not perfecting these nine essentials only makes their accomplishment that much more difficult. So there's no better time to begin than now.

So let's get started. Grab your clubs and let's head out to the range.

PART ONE

CREDIBILITY
Earning the Right to Lead Through Character

I hope I shall always have the firmness and virtue enough to maintain, what I consider the most enviable of all titles, the character of an honest man.

—*George Washington*

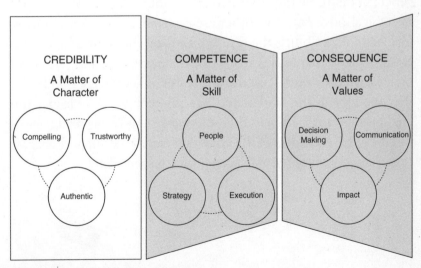

Figure P1.1. A Matter of Character

Leaders come to their leadership role along many pathways. Constituents elect them, they are appointed by the more powerful, they seize it from the weak or earn it through merit. Sometimes they volunteer to fill an existing void. Leaders also appoint themselves—when they start companies or organizations and declare it is they who will lead the effort.

But however they come to the task, they keep it—and become Unusually Excellent leaders—only if they continually earn the right to lead as granted by their most important followers, the "influencers" within the organization. On the one hand, lose the support of those value-creators and you face, at best, the dampened and sullen productivity of an unwilling team, and at worst, an active mutiny, or mass exodus of the most talented members. On the other hand, earn the right to lead from your best and brightest, and you will be rewarded with much more than simply compliance or obedience—you will gain true commitment, loyalty, and almost superhuman effort.

As the chapters that follow will highlight, leading on the field is largely a matter of *competence*, once you've earned the right to lead. There are a few rare leaders who have so much skill, intelligence, or charisma that they can create incredible loyalty in spite of some shortcomings in other areas—leaders like Bill Clinton. Leadership credibility, the result of earning the right to lead your team, is fundamentally a matter of *character*. Mother Teresa led purely from character—just the raw power of her presence and what she stood for in the world. The essential behaviors of leadership credibility—*being authentic*, *being trustworthy*, and *being compelling*—stand on the shoulders of the character traits that support each of them: *courage*, *integrity*, and *commitment*, respectively.

CHAPTER ONE

BEING AUTHENTIC
The Courage to Be Yourself

Self trust is the first secret of success.

—*Ralph Waldo Emerson*

He who knows others is wise. He who knows
himself is enlightened.

—*Lao Tzu*, The Tao Te Ching

B eing authentic—knowing who you really are, and holding true
to yourself in the most difficult moments—is "ground zero" of
leadership credibility. It all starts here, like taking your grip on a golf
club or tennis racquet—you must get step #1 right to ensure your
chances of success. To create the trusted connections you need to
lead with real influence, you must first pass the authenticity test of
your followers. It sounds simple but isn't; it takes courage, and there
are absolutely no trick plays or shortcuts.

I don't have to tell you that authenticity is more complicated
than simply "being yourself." For a very few people, this happens
without enormous effort, and they never think twice about it. But
for most leaders the complexity of their responsibilities creates the
occasional conflict that they must confront within themselves.
These are situations that test our ability to stay true to our core values in the face of tremendous temptation to take the easy way out.

Ask yourself: "When am I the most authentic?" The likely answer is when you are with family and close friends—the people with whom you can let down your guard and allow your true self to emerge.

What do those "authentic" moments have in common? *There is nothing at stake.* Your friends and family already know who you are, so being yourself with them has no unforeseen consequences. They know you aren't perfect, so you aren't obliged to be. They like you as you are, and they wouldn't want you any other way. When you are with these people in your life, you believe you are already inherently "good enough" to hold your place in that family, or that friendship. You aren't "trying out" anymore—you made the team, and you act like you know that. You trust yourself completely. There is no doubt in your mind that you are wholly and completely qualified.

These examples from the comfort of our lives with friends or family also illustrate the quality of the connection and ease of dialogue with others that we feel when there is no temptation to be someone we are not.

Although being ourselves authentically comes easily in most personal life settings, it is at times difficult as a leader for the other side of the same reason: when you are leading an organization, in the situations that test you the most, *there is usually something at stake*—for others and for you. The outcome of most leadership interactions has a consequence to everyone involved, and it is in your hands. These are the stressful times when you must have the courage of your convictions and be true to yourself in every way. These are the circumstances that challenge us to do the right thing even if it feels difficult, risky, or uncomfortable, and, in the same moment, tempt us to say something that just seems easier at the time.

Consider what is required to build that extra strand of muscle that most of us need to maintain our authentic self in a situation of meaningful consequence—where your decisions and conversations affect others, sometimes on a grand scale, and sometimes in very personal or dramatic ways. It takes an unusually insightful under-standing of yourself that is beyond what you would normally know without an extra effort. This is highly personal and disciplined work that most leaders will not attempt

Knowing who we are at the core is a project of awareness, courageous introspection, and thoughtful reflection. The inquiry we must embrace is: *What informs and creates our capacity to lead with real influence?* Surveys tell us we are informed by our own personal reflection—and it takes real courage to own the unvarnished truth about our lives and our past. We are also informed, in a profound way, by understanding how others perceive our leadership behavior. This requires a tolerance for unfiltered feedback that few leaders have. Let's look at each of these steps in detail.

Tale of Two Leaders: Polar Opposites

Here's a pair of stories, reflecting the antitheses of authenticity, from the part of my career as a venture capitalist. I've changed the names to protect the less-than-innocent.

Carl was the CEO of a venture-backed software company. He had previously held senior management positions at several large IT companies. He was the first kid in his family to go to college. He was well educated, with several graduate degrees. But he came from a family with humble roots in the Midwest. A classic story.

However, Carl never denied his roots. On the contrary, he *owned* them. The analogies he used in leading his team came from his life story; the things he chose to say in running the company were stories of his own from rural upbringing. He told them from the heart, and with great humility.

That humility was the most memorable thing about Carl. He knew who he was, and he understood what shaped him to be who he was. In the middle of Silicon Valley, he wore a cowboy hat and drove a pickup truck. And he didn't care whether you wore Brioni suits and drove a Lamborghini: he made no value judgments that way. And he felt no need to look like somebody else.

Where did this attitude come from? I think it went back to Carl's comfort with where he came from. In his world, there was no looking good, no keeping up with the Joneses, just a tight focus on getting it done. It was an upbringing that taught him to value excellence and experience. That's why Carl, who had a Ph.D., would emphasize a point not by reference to some academic theory, but rather with a story about working in the corn fields.

It was this realness, his what-you-see-is-what-you-get simple elegance, that became Carl's *platform for competence*. You never caught him acting like somebody he was not supposed to be. He was never trying to be someone he was not. This made him incredibly easy to talk with; you always felt like you were talking with the real person.

The effect of this way of behaving, consistently over time, is that, with his team, Carl enjoyed incredible trust and loyalty. People wanted to be on Carl's staff because his style was so authentic that he freed everyone to focus their energy on all the right things—and not worry about all of the overhead and excess calories of worrying about how you look and how you fit in. There was very little social currency that needed to be expended for the company to move forward. And you never, ever had to worry about competing with the boss.

From the unique perspective of being a substantial investor and director of the company during my time in that capacity, I began to notice something else: because Carl was so truthful about himself, you began to believe that he must also be equally truthful about the business. He started each board meeting with a financial overview demonstrating that he was on top of the economic viability of the company, and then he always gave an overview of what he was most worried about in the business, whether that was something internal or external to the operations of the company. We always knew what kept him up at night, so we knew where to focus our support. Carl used his board as a resource, trusting us with the real truth and therefore garnering tremendous respect. This is the kind of respect that every entrepreneur dreams of getting from investors, and he seemed to earn it effortlessly.

There was something else as well. I also noticed that when you were around Carl, his personal authenticity and honesty called you to a higher ground in your own behavior. Any phoniness or bombast on your part was thrown into sharp, embarrassing relief—and you backed down pretty quickly. This attitude made it possible to have board meetings that were remarkable in their combination of truthfulness, full disclosure, and open dialogue. You never felt *Ah, Carl's selling us one here*. Instead, his personal confidence allowed him to put bad news on the table without making it a judgment about his own worth. As you might predict, when it came to agreements, Carl was always as good as his word.

What made this even more impressive was that the company had only a moderately successful outcome. It was a niche business that never got to the scale we all had hoped for, and eventually it was sold for a good, but not great price to a large corporation. It was no grand slam; nobody really got rich from the years they spent at the company. Yet I suspect every one of them would join Carl again, no questions asked, if he called. I know that I would—because I know that the experience of working on Carl's team was so great that I almost didn't care what we were working on.

Now, in stark contrast, let me tell you about Bill, another entrepreneur whose company—this one based on the East Coast—I served, again as both an investor and a director.

Bill was also a brilliant guy—a trained corporate attorney—and his company had far more potential than Carl's in terms of both the available market and the potential financial gain for investors and employees. It was also a less complex and risky path to success than Carl's venture. But, tragically, Bill had made the conscious choice at some point in his career to adopt the then-popular notion of "leadership as performance"—and with that, he had transformed himself into the most inauthentic and ineffective leader I had ever encountered.

Some of this may have come from Bill's legal experience. Being an attorney is all about advocacy: gathering facts, conducting an analysis, and then developing the best case for your client to present with conviction and persuasion before a judge or jury. This is what we want from lawyers, but it isn't what we want from leaders. And that was Bill's fatal mistake.

His inauthentic, advocacy style created a bizarre kind of dog-and-pony culture inside Bill's company. For instance, the board would arrive at the board meeting wearing khakis and button-down shirts—and Bill would march in with his team, all in tailored suits. You could feel their attitude of OK, *time for the board performance*. Then Bill would take the stage, just like he was addressing the jury for an opening statement in a trial.

And that speech was always predictable in both its style and its substance. There was never a brutally truthful conversation about the state of the company. Rather, the message was always inspirational and hopeful—always *Field of Dreams* style—"If you build it, they will come." Bill never seemed to notice that by trying so hard to impress, to constantly reaffirm his leadership of the company, he was only making it obvious that he clearly wasn't comfortable in his own role. I can remember sitting there thinking: *Bill, why are you trying to sell yourself? You already got the job.*

This insecurity made it impossible for Bill to show any vulnerability with his team and his investors. He was constantly solving the problem, always on the brink of something great, defeating the competition. And implicit in these presentations was the sense that "If we can just get through this meeting, we can buy ourselves some time." Bill thought he was giving us what we wanted to hear, because he thought his job was to pacify and inspire the board—when in fact he was doing just the opposite.

And it only got worse. That same insecurity led Bill to fail at hiring people better than him for fear they would expose his weaknesses. Hiding in his suit of armor, he was much more comfortable keeping his B-team marching to his own drum beat. I believe he wasn't even conscious of doing this. And sometimes even that wasn't enough, so Bill would also overmanage his teams, lest they make a mistake and embarrass him.

What came next was almost inevitable. An ambitious guy, Bill had begun with a laser-like focus on success. In many ways it was his best quality. But before long, Bill abandoned that goal and became obsessed with merely failing elegantly—of not damaging his tender reputation. Ironically, the board of directors might have been able to help him—if only we had been given the real facts.

In the end, we had no real choice. We replaced Bill. By then it was an easy decision. Then the hard work began. We brought in a new CEO, who is still struggling to overcome a dysfunctional company filled with B-level talent working in a culture that rewards image over reality, gracefulness over victory—an organization of recovering codependents. It's going to be a long haul. As I write this, the fate of Bill's company, which once had the potential to be much greater and more famous than Carl's, is still up in the air.

For Bill, as you can imagine, being fired was devastating. His worst nightmare—what he had put on that elaborate show to prevent—had come true. How different the results would have been if he had just been authentic to himself and to others. And finally, knowing what I know now, and how fatal the disease of insecurity can be, I would never even consider investing in him again—or in anyone who even reminded me of him.

Look at Life: Seeing Who You Are

You must be willing to look at your life and reflect—on where you have been, what you have learned, and how your life experiences have shaped you—and realize that this collection of factors is now a meaningful and inescapable part of who you are and how you see the world. Listening to ourselves is difficult, and it doesn't occur to us in the normal course of a day—we are always thinking, moving from challenge to challenge, reacting, and getting things done. It is often true that the only thing we don't make time for is listening to ourselves—reflecting on our deepest thoughts, feelings, and intuitions. For some people, staying this busy is a way of permanently avoiding any self-reflection that would be possible. But that doesn't change its value. We need quiet time and personal space to search our memory for the patterns in our life that have become our routine. I'm convinced this is the purpose of six- or seven-hour flights where we have no obligation to others—just some time to think. We need to ask ourselves open-ended questions: Why did I do that yesterday? How do I feel about this, really? What worries me? What was I concerned about when I did that, or said that, or thought that? What is driving me right now? What past experience of mine just influenced my thoughts or feelings? This is work no one can do for you—you must initiate your own process and follow it through to your own insights.

This will not always be a comfortable set of reflections and thoughts. The painful memories will be even more instructive than the pleasant ones. In Steve Tappin's book *The Secrets of CEOs*, he reports that a large number of the CEOs he interviewed had suffered a trauma or had an adversity in their lives at one point that had significantly shaped their personal leadership philosophy. Everything we've done in life informs our outlook—both in ways we realize and, often, in ways we don't know—sometimes it is a tough lesson learned or the wisdom of a mentor along the way. It could even be a cliché or prejudice passed down from a parent or sibling that resonated so strongly that it has served as a guiding principle for us ever since—"Never go home before the people you work for," "Don't trust people from New York," and so on. Whatever these messages within us are, we need to find them within our deepest patterns of thought and to appreciate that they have, to one degree or another, shaped our point of view in life, probably unknowingly. We want the right to dismiss them as silly or even dangerous, but we must realize they are within us and locate them for a rigorous inspection.

The lens through which you see the world is uniquely yours; it affects the way you interpret everything that passes before you, and you must own that point of view and any biases that come with it. In fact, you must embrace it and allow others some insight as to how you see things from the experiences you've had. When we explain ourselves in terms of our background and the view of life it gives us, we invite others to see our perspective, and in a leadership relationship this is a big step toward creating a personal connection to our constituents. When we own our point of view publicly and take responsibility for seeing things the way we do, we allow debates and conversations to occur more objectively. We can separate the facts from the bias that we might carry and that keeps others from feeling as if they are fighting our "opinion." When the authority of hierarchy speaks with a strong personal opinion—as opposed to a strong fact-based point of view—it usually serves to shut down any hope of a useful, collaborative dialogue; no one wants to argue with the boss's "opinion." Unusually Excellent leaders also find opportunities to weave a lesson or principle from a specific experience from their life into a conversation or a situation as it occurs, as a way of further revealing some insight into what makes them tick.

We are who we are, and it is comforting to our teams to know something about our background—and that is possible only when we are willing to look at ourselves and see what is really there. When you, as a leader, are willing to explore the forces and events that shaped your point of view, the process results in the comfort of knowing you have reflected on your life story and accounted for the experiences that have formed your unique and personal point of view toward important ideas, concepts, and principles. Ultimately, knowing yourself better than you thought you could will repay you many times over in the form of the confidence that comes from being totally comfortable in your own skin. You can then move forward with a different kind of ease—knowing yourself at the core and understanding how you will approach and deal with the inevitable challenges of leadership. In the toughest moments, the one person who will always be there with you is—you. You want to know that person.

Owning Your Past: The Sting of Failure

Most of us in leadership positions live by the credo "Failure is not an option." Yet every successful business titan I've ever known has failed in his or her career at least once, usually miserably. But whereas mediocre leaders often spend their entire lives running from some past catastrophe, great leaders embrace those failures, carry the lessons with them, and continue to learn from them as they go. If self-reflection seems difficult, acceptance of failure will feel nearly impossible. There is a significant and natural resistance to including in your self-image the failures and shortcomings in your past. Executives who achieve great success are often, paradoxically, experts at marshalling the defenses required to avoid or resist the analysis of their failures and disappointments. They tend to ignore, deny, rationalize, or justify those events as something other than their responsibility. And they certainly don't want to talk about any of it publicly. Why? Simply because at many levels within their psyche, it serves them to avoid seeing the harsh truth. Because they'd have to admit to subordinates that they aren't perfect. Because they will disappoint some people in this moment in time—even though, in the long run, they are helping others form a more authentic understanding of the true person they are. Because, most of all, they will no longer have an excuse to offer themselves—that the failure really belongs not to them at the core of who they are, but to that other public persona that poorly represents them.

Success in this effort is measured by the degree to which you can accept what is really true about your history and the wins and losses contained therein. It requires a declaration to yourself that your past—all of it—is actually, legitimately OK. You accept who you are, what you've done, and the disappointments that come with life. You have forgiven yourself and others as necessary and left your resentments and anger at the door, and you have captured those lessons and included them in your current view of the world.

As a leader, if you do not make peace with these events from your history, you will forever be reliving them, and you will unconsciously infect your future with the unfinished business of the past. Of course, it is helpful to remember that all the other people you know have their stories, their disappointments, and their regrets. It is also useful to remind yourself of something we already know, but may have forgotten in an attempt to block out bad memories: that adversity often demands the best from us, and without these tough times we would not be who we are, in many of the ways in which we are best.

Adversity demands more of us than normal times do. There is a reason they call it a "learning experience," or a "character-building experience." Because challenge pushes us—and when we are pushed, and stretched, and challenged, we learn who we are and what we are made of. But sometimes that pushing, stretching, and challenging results in a failure or shortfall. And we must embrace those experiences and appreciate them as having helped us become who we are today—stronger for it all.

An Unexpectedly Bad Day

Consider the "learning experience" of professional golfer Dustin Johnson, at the 2010 United States Open Championship at Pebble Beach.

Johnson came into the 2010 U.S. Open as one of the hottest, most successful young players on the PGA Tour. He arrived at Pebble Beach with high hopes for a strong showing—he had won the last two PGA Tour events at the same golf course, the AT&T Pebble Beach Pro-Am tournaments in 2009 and 2010.

"Whenever you have success at a golf course, you get a lot of confidence," Johnson said. "So I've got a lot of confidence here. The first time I walked out here I loved the place. And I really enjoy playing golf here. You couldn't ask for a more beautiful place. And I just really enjoy it."

The three-time winner was also considered the best athlete on the PGA Tour, certainly one of the few able to dunk a basketball. But the question, as he faced his final round in the U.S. Open was—could he handle the immense pressure on a Sunday afternoon in his first legitimate chance to win a "major" and put his name on that trophy along with Jack Nicklaus, Arnold Palmer, Tom Watson, Tiger Woods, and many other legends of golf?

After a stunning 5 under par performance on Saturday, Johnson found himself sleeping on the lead Saturday night, and positioned in the last group on Sunday with Graeme McDowell, who was 3 shots behind Johnson's 6 under par total for the first three rounds. It was Johnson's tournament to win, and he looked invincible.

"I think I'm very patient most of the time," he said. "Sometimes I can get a little impatient, I'll hurry. But tomorrow I'll just try to keep it slow, keep a good routine going like I've been doing, and take what the golf course gives me.

"This is what I live for. This is what I practice every day for. This is why I go to the gym and do all the stuff that I do, to be in a position like this to go out and have a chance to win a U.S. Open."

Sunday did not turn out as Johnson wished—in fact, it was a long, slow-motion train wreck, with every painful mistake broadcast globally to sixty million viewers, complete with a harsh, but honest appraisal of Johnson's meltdown. The expert commentators showed no mercy in critiquing Johnson's unexpected technical flaws—which he had never before shown to be subject to—as well as his lapses in concentration and focus under the immense fishbowl pressure of playing in the last group in the U.S. Open at Pebble Beach. The mental and physical challenge to remain calm and find your best game in that crucible are beyond what most of us could possibly imagine.

Johnson started out badly Sunday, and it just got worse from there. His final-round 82 was the worst score by a 54-hole Open leader since 1911. This was not the distinction Johnson was hoping to earn. In short, it was a nationally televised character-building event for Dustin Johnson. It certainly tested both every fiber in his body and every promise he had made to himself to stay calm and "take it one shot at a time."

But the lesson of this story for leaders, in the midst of a chapter on *being authentic*, is to look at the opportunity it presented for Johnson to contextualize this substantial failure in his own authentic way and make his own decision and commitment about how this would shape his future.

After the round, when interviewed by the same analysts who had chronicled this embarrassingly miserable day for him, he said "Even though I played poorly today, I still had fun. I learned a lot. I'll get it done next time." We'll see if Johnson gets it done next time he is in a similar situation. The kind of outcome Johnson had at Pebble Beach that day will either inspire him to learn from his misfortune and go on to even greater accomplishments, or, as in the case of dozens of other players who've had similar experiences, crush his confidence forever.

Johnson took the exact right first step here. He accepted this disappointment for what it was—a bad day. In fact, to be clear, it was simply a day he did not execute as he had intended. It wasn't a bad strategy per se. And he is still the athlete and player he was before that day. He didn't allow it to be a negative statement about him or his talent or his accomplishments—rather, just about that round of golf. He spoke of it as a learning experience, and he vowed to come back stronger. This event is now part of his history, and he will own it. He can talk about it in a way that every 15 handicap weekend golfer can understand and empathize with, because they all have been there themselves—face to face with the cruelty of the game and unable to bring their best effort forward that day. He now has something that bonds him with every amateur partner he'll ever get in a Pro-Am.

Regarding disappointments like this one, it isn't what happens in our life that defines us, it is how we deal with it. It isn't whether we fall or not, but how we get up. Courage allows us to face our failures, and experience helps us deal with them. The next time Dustin Johnson is in a situation like the 2010 U.S. Open—if he is fortunate enough to be there again—you can be sure he'll be wiser, tougher, and more prepared to meet the challenge of that day. And he can credit himself for the way he accepted defeat with humility and learned everything he could, when a lesser man would be licking his wounds and blaming something outside himself.

Share the Shame

When you can appreciate the value of your failures and shortcomings as simply the lessons of life, no matter how painful they were at the time, another opportunity opens up. You now have a chance to pick the perfect moment and share with your team a story or two of your past disappointments, as a powerful way for you to connect with your followers on a personal level—with humility, which is a cornerstone of being authentic. Some leaders are tempted to hide behind their shame, using the authority of their position to justify it, and expect others to adhere to the philosophy "I am who I am—take it or leave it." This approach will most certainly get you what you deserve, which is a standoff with the folks you lead, with both sides camped in their corners of the ring, never to meet in the middle and share their experiences—and therefore never to connect, trust each other, and win together.

One of the reasons Cisco Systems survived the dot-com crash in 2000 and was prepared for the even bigger crash in 2009 was because chairman/CEO John Chambers had been a senior executive at Wang Labs, where he had watched helplessly as that billion-dollar corporation disintegrated and died. He carried that memory with him as both a warning lesson about management hubris and an object lesson in cash management—and it saved an even greater company.

Face Time

When Jim Wilson took over as CEO of a multibillion-dollar public company several years ago, the company was coming off some major setbacks including a stock repricing issue and a problem with restated earnings. These events threatened to derail the company from its leadership position within its industry.

It's the kind of situation that virtually demands a change of leadership—and Jim was the guy that the board of directors recruited away from a superb opportunity in his current role to turn this troubled company around.

There's a standard operating procedure for CEOs undertaking a major turnaround. You typically go in, keep a low profile for a couple months as you scope out the strengths and weaknesses of the operation and the key people, and then make your moves quickly and decisively.

But that is not what Jim did. Instead, he had another idea in mind for the beginning of his one-hundred-day plan. He spent his first three weeks with the company visiting the top (largest) ten employee locations—and keep in mind, it took a long time to reach all of them, as they were in Illinois, Arizona, Singapore, Japan, France, Italy, California, and Mumbai. During these first three weeks, he arrived at one of these locations late at night, and the next morning, he awoke at 5 A.M., drove to the local office or facility, and positioned himself at the entrance, where he served coffee and pastries to the entire employee population at that site. Jim stood at the front door of each location, dressed casually, and shook hands with every single employee entering the building. To each of them, he said, "Hi, I'm Jim Wilson. I'm the new CEO, and I'm happy to be part of the company. I hope to get to know you and learn about what you do." His goals were simple—model humility, authenticity, and availability, and give everyone in the organization personal access to him. At some locations this meant greeting over a thousand employees, which took more than six hours.

In other words, Jim began his tenure at the top of his new company not by meeting with the board, or hunkering down and reading reports, or even visiting customers. Instead, for almost his whole first month on the job, Jim did nothing else but introduce himself to *every* one of his employees, one-on-one and face-to-face. He made himself real on that cold, rainy Illinois dawn. And his message was: *I'm not above you, I'm with you. Thank you for letting me be a part of your company.*

In my experience, the best leaders always try to make that kind of personal connection with their followers. They make it a top priority, whereas less capable leaders do not—often because they just do not have that much interest in their subordinates as individuals. I know, from talking to others in Jim's company, that in all of the years before Jim's arrival, roughly 75 percent of the company's employees had *never* spoken with the CEO, much less shaken his hand. In fact, the previous CEO had never even shown up at three or four of the sites Jim visited within his first three weeks. Jim followed up his greeting of all the employees at the door with an all-hands, open-forum meeting at each site—and when possible, he brought his family along. He talked about his background, his successes and failures outside of "work," and the reasons that he had joined their company. He showed the team at each site the person behind the title "new CEO."

Jim did what most leaders are either too self-absorbed or too afraid to do: he connected with the entire team, as individuals, and realized that above everything else, they were all bound together by the things they all shared—being human and wanting to make a difference and be successful. Moreover, he was humble enough to go *to* his employees, not the other way around. And the resulting connection was sufficiently unique and personal to be compelling— indeed, unforgettable—for the employees. In the process, Jim and his new followers made an enduring *connection*—one that would soon show up in the company's results.

The Perception Gap

Although it is essential to know yourself in order to be authentic, it is equally important to know how others see you, so you can have that information to create the option of correcting the things that you may unknowingly be doing to undermine your good intentions and efforts—and potential success. Although self-knowledge is a great asset in knowing how you will interpret a situation or why you will react a certain way to an event, the feedback you can get from a diverse group of your constituents—if you try—will help you connect to your team on their terms, which are the only terms that matter to them.

All of us know that once we step out from behind our public persona, the real person we are is not always exactly the real person we want to be or hope we are. To be authentic is to face the truth about yourself as seen by others, and that can be a soul-shattering experience in a job where we want—indeed, almost need—to be admired and revered. Never forget that others' perceptions of you are their absolute reality, and it doesn't matter whether you know their views—they exist nonetheless, and it certainly isn't relevant whether or not you agree with what they see or feel. The gap between their reality and your self-image can be the cause of great frustration and even failure in key relationships across an organization.

Why do so few leaders get useful feedback? *Two* main reasons:

1. *Very few seek the feedback in a sincere and genuine fashion.* They really don't want to face the facts of how they are perceived. It can threaten a leader's self-esteem and self-image, not to mention whatever illusion the leader holds about his or her public reputation. Subconsciously, we may not want to hear the data we fear exists in our followers' world, and it may be more important to keep our self-confidence, no matter how much that keeps us locked in a delusional fantasy about our true standing. It's easy to talk about wanting feedback on your decisions, but it takes real guts to go out and seek comparable feedback on yourself. It really is easier to assume—or pretend—that everything is fine.

In the 1992 movie *A Few Good Men*, in a well-known scene, Colonel Nathan R. Jessep (played by Jack Nicholson) is on the witness stand, being cross-examined by Lieutenant Kaffee, a young attorney played by Tom Cruise. Kaffee is peppering Jessep with tough questions. Jessep finally loses his patience, and temper, and in a violently heated manner he blasts Kaffee: "You want answers?"

Kaffee replies with matching emotion, "I want the truth!"

Jessep snaps, "You can't handle the truth!"

This scene has become modern leadership folklore because it highlights exactly the fundamental issue in seeking feedback—*can we really handle the truth?* And, knowing how unpleasant it can be, most leaders in a position of substantial authority and power simply opt out of this exercise, preferring to carry on, doing what they hope works, but without the value of knowing, truly, the perceptions of themselves held by those they lead.

2. *Even if you have the guts to seek feedback, and believe you can handle it, it is difficult to get.* Leaders live in a protected space—a bit of a bubble, often surrounded by lots of yes-men who believe it is advantageous to stroke their leader's ego with wonderfully supportive "feedback" intended more to enhance the chances of their own advancement than to serve the growth of their boss. That's because to get the truth, you must pierce the nice, warm, insular bubble of ass-kissing bullshit that serves to delude many leaders into believing they are more positively perceived than they really are. You must seek feedback well beyond your circle of admiration, be it legitimate or politically motivated. Most important, you have to do anything you can to make it legitimately and completely safe for others to communicate their real experience of you. In most feedback summaries I've seen, leaders tend to overestimate the regard others have for them—and it is an understandable tendency. Specifically, the area in which leaders are overly optimistic is in their assumption of having created a trusting workplace—we'll deal with this topic in the next chapter.

Classic 360 degree review processes are generally useful, but sometimes misleadingly harsh, as anonymous feedback can degrade into a projection of the reviewer's own personal issues, so you have to look for themes, trends, and broad perceptions. Like the scores in an ice skating competition, it may be smart to throw out the high and the low and look for the data that defines the central message in each area.

However, if you are willing and able to get this precious feedback, the real value comes in hearing it constructively and committing to use it *diagnostically* to improve your leadership impact. First, try your best to depersonalize it. It usually isn't about *you* but about what you *do*. And it is just information. Try to see this feedback like the oil gauge in your car, or the reading on your home thermostat, which you would never confuse as something personal. The fact is that most of your constituents are not qualified to assess you in technical, psychological terms—what they are really reporting is their *experience* of working with you or for you. Finally, remember that it is difficult, if not impossible, for others to separate their historical biases and prejudices from the data that is uniquely about their experience of your leadership. Take it seriously, but remember, it isn't totally objective, and it isn't perfect. The more instructive opportunity of this data is to look for trends or consistency among groups of people—it is noteworthy to know the common perceptions of a larger sample of your followers.

Also, do your best to minimize the emotion and drama of the feedback. It is leadership *performance* feedback—you want it to do your job better. Ask for feedback specifically about your *behavior* as a leader—that is what you want. What do you *do* that works, and what do you *do* that doesn't work? Allowing the critique to wander into more personal territory, although instructive to know in some ways, opens a can of worms that ends up creating more problems than it solves. This is a business, not a marriage. Making it overly personal keeps you from hearing the useful part about your performance as a leader.

You will earn a significant level of respect for seeking this feedback, but you may never be acknowledged publicly for the courage that everyone knows this takes. I overheard our college-age son critiquing several professors with a friend, and was pleasantly surprised to learn that from his point of view, the teachers who asked for feedback more frequently, like once or twice during the term, were substantially more respected than the ones who waited until the end of the course to request their evaluations from the students—when the information was useless for improving that student's experience of the teaching. The feedback will also get better and better each time you ask for input, as your team realizes there is no penalty for giving you the information you wanted. Your willingness to hear this data counteracts the "ivory tower" or "asleep at the switch" prejudices that often distort followers' perceptions of their leaders—and are normally fully justified by their experience of other bosses along the way.

The Courage to Listen

I've already mentioned John Chambers of Cisco. There's another story about him that is related by journalists. At the end of an interview, John will ask the reporter, "How was that? How did I do? Did I answer all of your questions? Is there anything I can do better?"

First-time interviewers are often shocked by those questions. Fortune 50 CEOs are supposed to be Masters of the Universe, utterly confident in their dealings with the media, shareholders, and legislators. Moreover, by all accounts, Chambers is not indulging in some technique to ingratiate; he is honestly soliciting suggestions for how he can be better at his job—and he's not going to let pride get in the way of that education. It is no mystery that John is one of the very best CEOs on the planet with the media—he is likely one of the few who regularly seeks feedback on his effectiveness and includes it in his personal growth plan.

To my mind, one of the greatest stories of modern business is the Great Return of Bill Hewlett and Dave Packard. By the late 1980s, both men, having built one of the most admired American companies, had retired to board positions at their company. And by every important indicator the HP they had left behind was doing fine.

And yet, as the legend goes, Packard received a private memo from a longtime, low-level employee he'd never met, which warned him that—no matter what he heard from senior management—Hewlett-Packard was heading for the rocks.

I can't imagine that there have ever been more than a handful of big companies with cultures that would have emboldened an employee to write so forthrightly to the chairman of the board without fear of consequences. And I can think of only one company—HP under Bill and Dave—in which the chairman would actually read that letter, hear it as constructive feedback, and act on its message. In fact, within days, Dave Packard was grabbing every HP employee and contractor he could and soliciting their opinions on the company and his own stewardship. Based on what he heard, Packard, with Hewlett's support, turned HP upside down—and restored it to historic levels of success.

The Great Return could never have happened had Bill and Dave not spent the previous forty years building and reinforcing trusted and safe communications channels that empowered rank-and-file HP employees to speak honestly and forthrightly to the men at the very top of the company. It also would not have happened had Dave Packard refused to admit his own mistakes, or silenced the bad news, or allowed his pride to get in the way. Instead, he admitted that having been asleep at the switch, he had allowed the famous HP Way to become more a series of meaningless rituals than a living corporate culture, and most of all, he had let HP grow old, stuffy, and slow. Packard showed that he could handle the truth, even at the cost of his own perfect image.

Honest Feedback

Although this effort to gather honest, useful feedback is difficult, private, and personal, and can be upsetting and disruptive, it is the work that separates Unusually Excellent, unusually credible leaders from the rest of the pack. If you are willing to do it with vigor and sincerity, you'll minimize the chance that your credibility will ever be limited by your own shortage of self-knowledge, self-acceptance, or self-confidence. The vast majority of leaders work in the illusion that they know how they are perceived in their organizations, and therefore they believe they know what works about their leadership. They are often dramatically out of touch with reality within their organizations. It is the rare leader who wants and gets the feedback that could move the leader from the ranks of the "normal" to the classification "extraordinary"—if the leader only knew what followers really thought about him or her.

Being authentic 100 percent of the time is a high bar, but it is the appropriate goal for leaders, and theoretically it should be a simple objective to achieve. But most of us are not perfect in our track record on this topic, and sometimes we find ourselves in situations that truly test our mettle. Why are we tempted to slide from what we wanted to do, or say, to the point where we compromise the authentic leader we would so much prefer to be? I think there are four basic reasons—most of which we simply don't notice in our own behavior at the moment we stumble. The pitfalls to watch for are as follows:

- *We feel insecure and we get scared.* Yes, even tough-guy and tough-gal leaders are subject to self-doubt at times. We can be caught off-guard, face-to-face with a tough or tricky leadership situation, and feel unprepared. Or we find ourselves in a circumstance where we aren't sure how it will turn out, and we can't tolerate the anxiety of the unpredictable outcome. We may imagine negative consequences for being brutally honest at the moment—and so we lose faith in ruthless candor as the right approach to the situation. At that point, we actually believe another path of action would serve us better—or at least it feels like that for the moment, and we take the bait. We start down a road that feels easier, and we can't find an exit. We protect ourselves.

- *We know what to say, but we don't know how to say it "right."* We know what must be said, and we'd like to say it, honestly and authentically, without being harsh or inflammatory. But we don't know exactly how to get the right conversation started. We assume it can't be done—that we can't communicate with both total honesty and empathetic compassion. So we opt for what feels feasible or what we've said before in a similar situation—and it usually isn't exactly what we wanted to say.

- *We take on other people's feelings*—or what we imagine their feelings will be—and we make them ours. Then we get lost or confused in the emotion of the situation—and ultimately we lose

ourselves to others' concerns and become codependent in the occasion. We opt for taking care of others' feelings now and sacrificing
the truth that we know we must deal with later.

• *We want to avoid the emotional pain of conflict* that a brutally
honest communication might cause—so we get into the habit of
exchanging the short-term advantages of compromise for the long-
term consequences of being inauthentic. We all avoid pain if
possible—but it just isn't the best tactic if it compromises the basic
values that we stand for. Take your pain quickly and acutely. Learn
to be comfortable with discomfort—and surprisingly, it does get
easier after a few times through. It just becomes habitual to be
authentic—or inauthentic. Habits are the things we repeatedly do.

The awful truth is that most of us compromise our authenticity,
in small and not-so-small ways, more frequently than we'd want to
admit to anyone, especially ourselves. And each time we do so, it
is a paper cut to our self-respect. And people in power and authority are no more immune than anyone else—perhaps less so, given
the ever-present pressure to appear all-knowing. The temptation to
say or do something "easier" than what we know is necessary is, at
times, intense. Our authenticity, and the courage that supports it, is
tested in moments like these.

When we shortchange our integrity in this fashion, we are essentially making a decision that we don't think we can be "be ourselves"
or "say our truth"—for the reasons just outlined. In turn, this usually
results in delivering a message that isn't truly what we wanted or
needed to say. In that moment, we imagine that saying something
that was easier to say but isn't what we meant will magically increase
our options, decrease our discomfort, or smooth the path to action,
avoiding something awkward or painful, or protecting our real selves
from potential backlash or failure. Deception conspires with fear and
seduces us down a dark road of believing we can "fake it," just this
one time, and it will all be OK.

But the downstream impact of making such a choice in a
moment of stress or carelessness can be devastating. It always comes

home to roost. For one thing, it compromises the integrity of that all-important communications channel between leader and followers by changing expectations about the behavior of both. Worse, it sets a precedent for this type of inauthentic behavior that over time can trap a leader into an expectation or pattern of *always* behaving this way—over the course of years, a soul-destroying situation.

That's why the higher you go in an organization—and the more power and status you hold—the *greater* the value of authenticity. Many things are amplified at the top of the leadership pyramid, and authenticity is one of the two things it is most dangerous for us to compromise. (See Chapter Two, Being Trustworthy, for the other one).

However, the rewards for leading an organization with authenticity are enormous. Mainly, it opens the door and invites in so many of what the ancients considered to be the classic virtues: humility, security, self-knowledge, thoughtfulness, mindfulness, connectedness, approachability, curiosity, and accountability— basically, all the things you wish you could see in the people who have led or now lead *you*. Further, it allows for the personal connections with people across the organization that are so critical to being broadly known and respected.

At the same time, authenticity acts as a natural immunity—like a vaccine—to the occupational diseases that accompany the game of power and that plague many leaders, such as aloofness, narcissism, isolation, the tendency to be surrounded by "yes men," and disconnectedness. It also tends to strengthen the good kind of ego—confidence, while undermining the bad kind—arrogance.

In other words, when you can call on the courage to show your true self, with all of your warts and scars and shortcomings, for the world at large to witness, it's pretty hard to be a pompous ass to the people who want your guidance, support, and direction the most.

Unusually Excellent leaders strive to remain self-aware and authentic in an environment designed to protect them from bad news about the organization and themselves. They spend a considerable amount of their time and energy staying grounded and connected, despite all of the institutional filters. They know that information becomes unreliable at altitude (higher up the organization), perpetually stuck a level below where it is needed most—so they develop techniques to end-run those barriers and liberate the truth, no matter how painful it is to hear.

The best leaders remember that although no one at the top can completely escape being seen by others as the "boss," they can find ways to relate at a human level with their followers, from informal gatherings to spontaneous visits. They seek out and cultivate employees at all levels who will speak to them with real candor. And they consciously present themselves as accessible and open and vulnerable—that is, they talk about their fears, challenges, and failures with humility, candor, and at times even some humor—so as to break down the barriers with those whom they wish to know. It is the mark of great leaders to know how to communicate with extraordinary authenticity and still be completely professional and appropriate given the specific circumstances, context, and appreciation of the authority they hold within the organization.

Breathe and Be Yourself

Authenticity is the first step of leadership greatness because it is the basis for the kinds of trusting relationships with followers that are crucial for taking on demanding tasks that lead to notable accomplishments. It also serves to humanize and soften the positional power that accompanies the built-in authority of senior leadership. But authenticity is also, in my experience, one of the most difficult aspects of leadership for even the most secure, experienced, successful leaders to fully grasp and own. Digging into this paradox yields fascinating insights and some practical ideas for leaders to master something that ostensibly should be easy, but isn't: being themselves—*always*—and owning and embracing their own personalities, flaws, fears, passions, and values while still providing the role model behavior that is expected of them in a position of leadership accountability.

But it can be done—and we have the examples of great leaders before us to show us how to do it. Authenticity is rarely a neutral experience for our followers—if we are indeed authentic in the whole of our leadership behavior, it will be a huge asset in our credibility and effectiveness. If, however, we fall short of our followers' expectations in this crucial area, or we attempt to "role-play" an authentic leader when we are not, it will be a gigantic liability, and our credibility will be hamstrung indefinitely by this deficiency. It is almost this black-and-white, and it is worth the work it takes to get it right. The authentic leader ultimately has a happier, more fulfilling, and more successful career. Authentic leaders *win*.

In the end, perhaps the greatest contribution that communication makes to authenticity is not that it warns us when we are fooling *others*, but that it reminds us when we are fooling *ourselves*.

The Essentials of Being Authentic

- Just do it. Invest in yourself by doing the work you must do to truly know who you are—your life story, the things that shaped you, and your disappointments and failures. Own yourself for who you really are. This is what allows others to connect. There is no one who can do this work for you.

- Trust the power of allowing others to know you. Even though it can seem scary, and it requires the willingness to be vulnerable, it is the key to influence. The real you—no imitations or role-playing—is what people want to know, and the real you is the person to whom they will commit.

- Find the courage to be yourself when the pressure of leadership tempts you otherwise. There is nothing more comforting to others, especially in times of stress, than to realize that you know and trust yourself.

- Declare yourself worthy, adequate, and deserving of the job you have. Don't doubt yourself if you expect others not to.

- Be careful about "trying" too hard to be authentic. Being yourself should feel easier than being the image you think others want of you. Don't be authentic in the way someone else is—do it your way.

- Seek feedback from a wide group of your followers. Try to use it diagnostically, to improve, not as a threat to your self-image, self-esteem, or self-worth.

- Stand on personal courage to create relationships. You will be rewarded with loyalty.

CHAPTER TWO

BEING TRUSTWORTHY
The Consistency of Integrity

If any man seeks for greatness, let him forget
greatness and ask for the truth, and he will
find both.

> —*Horace Mann*

If you tell the truth, you don't have to remember
anything.

> —*Mark Twain*

Lieutenant-General Robert Baden-Powell became famous during the Boer War for successfully, and with great resourcefulness, leading the British Army under siege at Mafeking.

But Lord Baden-Powell gained a kind of immortality a decade later when he founded the Boy Scouts. It is not a coincidence that, when it came time to write the tenets of the Scout Law, Baden-Powell chose to put "trustworthy" first. It is still there, a century later.

In Chapter One we began a logical progression that we will continue to build on throughout this book. So far, it goes like this: Unusually Excellent leaders find the courage within to be authentic—and that takes knowing themselves, accepting the disappointments of their past, and actively seeking feedback from their teams.

In this chapter, we learn that they follow this essential commitment to authenticity with a promise to be *trustworthy*—to build a
track record of honesty, fairness, and integrity that creates a leadership "equity" within their constituency. This is the currency
they need when it becomes necessary to make unreasonable
performance demands on their teams. In subsequent chapters
we'll show how this equity empowers trustworthy and authentic
leaders to use their moral authority to inspire the highest-quality
execution from their teams, as well as to carry those teams
through extreme challenges and failures.

Why is trustworthiness so important in the life of a leader that
it takes precedence over heavyweight attributes like creativity and
intelligence? Why is trustworthiness the most noble of all of the
attributes of leadership? For the answer, I could refer you to three
thousand years of philosophical writings about the nature of
honor and trust. But this book is about the necessary steps to great
leadership—and for that, I'll give you some very pragmatic and
strategic reasons why you should commit yourself to cultivating
and protecting your reputation for trustworthiness.

Poisoned Ground

However, before we outline the steps to get there, let's first discuss
the environment around trust that most leaders inherit from
decades of the behavior of the leaders who preceded them. That is,
it is instructive to remind ourselves of the climate from which trust
has emerged as such a crucial, but often misunderstood cornerstone
for the development of leadership equity.

Leadership is almost always accompanied by some degree of
organizational authority that, in its most basic form, is a close proxy
for "power"—a power that can be, and likely has been, used against
most people in the workplace, either purposefully or inadvertently.
In either case, it would be safe to say that authority, and the power
that accompanies it, has probably done some damage to most people. Most people have been harmed at some point by the hand of

power in an organization—that power being falsely presented as "leadership" or "benevolent authority." Perhaps it was an unjust firing, an unwarranted inquiry, or an ungrounded accusation.

So leadership or "management," as a euphemistic label for authority or power, has acquired a mixed reputation at best. Leaders should assume that the starting condition for many people in an organization is a mildly to significantly negative experience of leadership—the damage stemming mostly from having trusted those in power and subsequently being used, abused, disappointed, or hurt. The conclusion many people have formed, based on their experience, is that most organizations are inherently unsafe. So this history, including the wounds of power, is alive and visible in followers in the form of distrust, skepticism, or even cynicism. Add to this the myriad examples in most of our lives of personal disappointment or hurt from trusting others, and you have a double whammy: "trust" can be a bad word—and one that may be sold in a bottle labeled "leadership."

As leaders we must overcome this prejudice—this distrust of authority that makes the task of creating trusting environments even more challenging. It is difficult enough to start this work from zero, but in most organizations, leaders are in negative territory before they begin. We must transcend our followers' fears of organizational power and ensure that our teams can experience real leadership. The thoughtful and even-handed authority that comes with skilled leadership can—and should—be a trustworthy, positive experience. If we miss this chance, history repeats itself, this prejudice persists, and a real leadership experience is delayed for another generation. This is a cycle of neglect that only Unusually Excellent leaders can break.

So with the challenge of these starting conditions as a cold wind in our face, we remind ourselves that although it is an uphill climb, failure is not an option. We must rise above the resistance, the apathy, or the suspicion and lead the dialogue that creates the experience of trust in our organizations—that is the essential prerequisite to the organizational culture we need to create remarkable results.

To my mind there is absolutely nothing more important than a leader's trustworthiness. As anachronistic as it may sound in the twenty-first century, men and women whose word is their honor, and who can be absolutely trusted to be fair, honest, and forthright, are more likely to command the respect of others than any other type of person. That said, a trustworthy leader doesn't have to be a Boy Scout or even a good or kind person—on the contrary, history teaches us that some of the most trustworthy people can be harsh, tough, or socially awkward people—but their promises must be inviolate and their decisions fair.

Safely Successful

Trust is arguably the most important element of organizational effectiveness. To attempt to achieve the goals most organizations strive for without a culture of trust is not impossible, but it is immeasurably more difficult, and it only adds to the formidable challenges inherent in the market. Leaders must initiate the trust-building process with their own commitment to trustworthy behavior. Let's hit the two main points of this topic:

What is the fundamental purpose of trust?

How do leaders build trust in organizations?

What is the essence of trust? Trust is about safety. The presence of trust, in organizations, creates the feeling of confidence—a secure knowledge that our behavior, our work, and our performance will be evaluated in an objective, rational, and consistent way. It means we need not fear a subjective, arbitrary, or personal attack that would threaten our reputation or stability within the organization—or worse, our self-esteem. We can then manage ourselves accordingly. It is the comfort of knowing we'll be treated fairly if we simply do the right thing. What solidifies this feeling of safety is experiencing it consistently, to the point where it is *predictable*. We can count on it. Then, and only then, are we freed up, and fired up to do our best work.

There is a primal, biological need in all of us to feel safe—physically, emotionally, and professionally. When we don't feel safe, our natural response is to focus energy toward a showdown with the perceived threat—and our attention on whatever scares us will increase until we either fight or run, in the other direction, or the threat diminishes on its own. It will certainly distract us from what we cared about before we got scared. In a jungle or a dangerous dark alley, this threat is visceral; in business or organizations, it is masked or subtle; but the response is the same: distraction, fear, and, at the extreme, paralysis. And that response is hidden inside "business" behaviors—sandbagging quotas, hedging on stretch goals, avoiding accountability or commitment.

How do we build a trustful place for our followers? Most important, as Barry Posner writes in *Leadership Challenge*, as a leader, when it comes to building trust you must "go first"—you must *model the way*. Being trustworthy creates trust. Don't wait for others to demonstrate their trustworthiness for you to trust them. That is a silly game of cat-and-mouse that can go on indefinitely, with both parties waiting for the other to earn their trust. It is the leader's job to step up and start the process by granting trust up front and allowing others to earn that trust later through their behavior. Leaders take the risk. That is why they are leaders.

So how do leaders tackle this challenge head-on, starting the process themselves to create the trustful environment that everyone wants? There are slightly different tactics to focus on interpersonal trust building and its cousin, organizational trust. Let's look at each separately.

No Tricks Here; Just the Basics, Done Well

There are some very simple but powerful things every leader can do to increase his or her trust level with anyone—or everyone—in the organization. It is not the complexity or difficulty of the following suggestions that will challenge leaders. It is the awareness and discipline to actually do them consistently. This stuff is not, as they say, rocket science. But you can't reap the rewards if you don't sow the seeds of the effort to improve these behaviors.

• *Be honest.* Tell the truth, match your actions with your words, and match those words with the truth we all see in the world: no spin, no bullshit, no fancy justifications or revisionist history—just tell the truth. Telling the truth when it is not convenient or popular, or when it will make you look bad, can be tough—but is essential to your reputation. When you feel yourself starting to bend what you know is the truth, find a way to stop, reformat your communication, and tell the truth. It is hard to overstate the power of honesty. This behavior alone creates trust.

• *Be vulnerable.* We trust people we believe are real (authentic) and also human (imperfect and flawed)—just like us. And that usually means showing others some vulnerability—some authentic (not fabricated) weakness or fear or raw emotion that allows others to see us as like them and therefore relate to us at the human level. Relating is a requirement for trusting. We don't relate to people whom we feel are substantially better than or different from us, especially if those people try too hard to appear perfect.

• *Be fair.* This begins at the top. If you treat your followers fairly, and do so consistently, you will set a pattern of behavior for the entire organization. This sense of fairness, critical to the creation of a safe environment, can be reinforced not only by complimenting fair practices but also by privately speaking to—or if necessary, censuring—subordinates who behave unfairly to others in the organization. Precise agreements about what is fair are hard to negotiate, because each of us has our own sense of fairness when it is specifically about us. But at the level of general principle there is seldom any confusion about what fair looks like. Just ask yourself: would most people see this as fair or unfair? And don't confuse the idea of "not what I wanted" with "not fair." Leaders get paid to know and speak to this difference.

Implied Distrust

One dishonest behavior by leaders seems so obviously wrong that I'm constantly appalled they still try to get away with it. I'm talking about what might be called the "adulterer's guarantee." This example illustrates a general point—the moment you think your power or authority in an organization authorizes you to behave dishonestly and abusively, you have just initiated your own credibility destruction project.

Here's how it happens. A person comes to you and says, "I just lied to [someone else], but you can trust *me* because I'd never lie to you." Shockingly, this happens more often than you might realize—almost always in very subtle or disguised ways. What I want to discuss now is the impact this behavior has on a leader's credibility and reputation for trustworthiness.

To do that, I want to tell you a story—one in which the players are so famous that I definitely need to disguise their names.

On the team of the chief marketing officer (CMO) of one of the fastest-growing technology companies on the planet there was a young, somewhat inexperienced, but talented associate who had what he thought was a plan for a powerful new marketing initiative. The associate courageously asked the CMO to broker a meeting with the CEO to make a presentation on the subject. The CMO agreed. He felt a moderate loyalty to the young associate—not enough to fall on his sword for him, but enough to be willing to open the door. And he respected the associate's chutzpah for wanting the meeting with the big boss. The CMO used his relationship with the CEO to broker this meeting, and soon it was on all of their calendars.

The presentation itself, which took a half-hour, was attended by just the three of them. The CEO, because he came from a marketing background, had the expertise and arrogance to do a real-time critical analysis of the presentation—and the CMO could tell early on that the presentation wasn't going well. Indeed, it was going quite badly, for reasons that he hadn't anticipated.

Still, the CEO was polite, if noncommittal. He gave the presenter a sort of passively accepting feedback—"Nice point," "Interesting," and so on—and wrapped up the meeting quickly, thanking the presenter for his initiative. But the CMO could sense a duplicity in the CEO's behavior and attitude as the parties all headed back to their respective offices.

Up to that point, this was like a million other presentations that take place every day in the business world. But then, predictably, ten minutes after the meeting, the CEO called the CMO into his office and said, in essence, "That presentation was absolutely terrible. That guy's an idiot. I want you to fire him, today."

Let's pause for a moment and look at all of the relationships that had just been compromised by the CEO's cowardly behavior. First, and most obviously, the presenter, who believed he was doing his best to help the company and got reasonable feedback from the CEO at the time, was to be rewarded for his loyalty by being summarily dismissed—which would certainly be a traumatic event at this stage of his young career. The CMO, who had merely acted as an interme-diary, found himself charged with firing one of his own people for rea-sons he didn't completely understand or agree with—and had to decide whether he should take responsibility for that decision or tell the truth: that it was the CEO's emotional reaction that had created the situation. And he had to make this choice *immediately*, although he was still disappointed with the presenter and angry at the CEO for putting him in this position—and still worried about the damage to his own reputation for endorsing the meeting.

But most of all, the CMO was left wondering—having seen the CEO so comfortably being passive-aggressive and two-faced—whether he could ever trust his words again. In the future, when the CEO expressed his approval to the CMO, how could he not won-der whether the CEO wasn't actually ordering his termination at someone else's hands?

Such is the nature of trust. The CEO should have had the courage during the meeting to say, "Hey, this is not a good presentation. This is not what we wanted. It is not that I don't like you, but I am disappointed in the quality of this work. I want to give you my honest opinion—I'm not sure we can recover from this." That would be called leadership.

Instead, the CEO hid behind his authority, misrepresented his true feelings, and had a subordinate do his dirty work. Had the CEO showed courage and been authentic to his true feelings, the crisis would have ended right there. The marketer might still have lost his job—but he would have left thinking *Well, I just didn't make it here*. Instead, he left thinking *This place is a disaster, and the CEO is a liar*. Meanwhile, the story of the firing spread (as it always does) throughout the company, morale slipped, and the CMO never completely trusted his boss again. The CEO's reputation for trustworthiness had been wounded forever. The wreckage from one seemingly small act of dishonesty was strewn all over the company and could never be completely cleaned up.

Should I Believe You?

Here's a quick, but I think telling, anecdote that illustrates how trustworthiness includes doing what you say you are going to do.

There's a company I know in which the CEO had one executive on his team whom he really trusted and in whom he could confide.

One day, a couple of other members of that company's executive team made a presentation at a board meeting that didn't go well. Later, as they were walking down a hallway, the CEO turned to his trusted executive and said, "We need to get rid of those guys. They were a disaster at the board meeting—they embarrassed me."

But then nothing happened. Life at the company went on as before, and the targeted executives remained in their jobs. In the months that passed, the trusted executive found himself in meetings attended by both the CEO and the targeted executives.

And it was as if the whole incident had never happened. The CEO joked with the men, complimented them on their work, and treated them as long-term team members.

As the trusted executive watched this, he asked himself: *Did the boss mean what he said? Does he ever mean what he says? Did he change his mind—and when did that happen? Or is he too gutless to follow through with his plans? And if he's willing to stab those guys in the back and then pretend to be their trusting partner, how do I know he hasn't been doing the same thing with me? Just how duplicitous is this guy?*

For the trusted executive, the landscape of the company had been irreparably changed by this sudden lightning bolt of distrust. Luckily for the CEO, the executive had more honor than his boss, and he didn't spread the story through the company. Such are the dangers of shooting from the hip without realizing that a communication such as the one just described does not qualify as a "casual" comment—once said, it must be resolved, and if it is not, there is a lingering odor that, in one way or another, will remain smelly until fixed.

Trust starts with one-on-one interactions and proceeds to group interactions and conversations in which followers integrate and confirm their personal experience with leaders in a group setting. Ideally, leaders can establish some additional "equity" with key individuals that can be leveraged as they move to creating organizational safety.

There are some tangible results you will notice when you are successful in creating higher interpersonal trust. The attributes we desire in trusted interpersonal relationships—and that you really want *more* of over time (you can never have too much)—are as follows:

- *Relationship*—a sense of real connectedness and mutual respect marked by open, honest communication
- *Commitment*—an explicit promise to work with conviction toward the goals you share
- *Loyalty*—an unspoken agreement that you are in this together, will be there for each other, and certainly would not surprise the other person with your departure

In addition, you will likely see a growth in the connections between people that hold things together under stress and pressure— a feeling of stability. It is the confidence that we can count on people to be there; to do the right things and to do them as well as they possibly can.

A Better Place for All

Interpersonal relationships are the building blocks for broader organizational trust. The stories of trustworthy behavior will make their way through the organization and create the conditions for a fabric of trust to be woven—and will show up in the nature of the dialogue in large meetings and group conversations, where the conversation moves beyond the bond between individuals. To move trust building from a one-to-one focus to the broader culture, there are some other things you can do that apply specifically to organization-level trust dynamics.

• *Do anything you can to reduce fear of irrational consequence.* Fear in the organization impedes the flow of useful information and compromises the integrity of the truthfulness of the data in ways both subtle and spectacular. Bad news moving "up" the organization is an acute manifestation of this problem. If you want to determine how much fear there is in the organization, get the answers to these two key questions:

How fast does bad news travel?

How hard is it to locate the facts?

Fear inspires defensive behavior, and when people are scared their attention shifts from investing their energy in their work to protecting or defending their image or reputation. Talk out loud about your commitment to creating a safe place for the truth to live—and walk your talk on this one.

• *Have a bias for disclosure, and be transparent.* All great enterprises have a free flow of data from top to bottom, with a minimal amount of political friction. Needless to say, this is both the product and the source of institutional trust. Again, this starts at the top. Your task as leader is to be as forthright and transparent as is realistically possible, with full and regular communications to all of your followers. Strive to disclose the maximum amount of information appropriate to the situation. Allow others access to the underpinnings of important decisions and communications. Provide the context that lets the team know that they can be trusted to see how things are done, decisions are formulated, and strategies are created—and that this won't be done in the dark with no explanations. The hoarding of valuable data within an organization to obtain power or influence can be devastating to that organization's effectiveness, and its long-term health.

• *Be clear.* Be as crystal clear as humanly possible, and be equally simple—when appropriate—in your communications, whether it be to one person or the whole of your team. Confusion creates anxiety, and anxiety is the beginning of fear. We are often not heard or understood as clearly as we think we have spoken. Ask others whether you were clear and what they understood you to say—then correct the communications, if necessary, and add an apology if the message you intended did not transmit. Clarity is foundational to trust. Let your behavior model your commitment to clarity, and you'll soon find others with a similar focus on being clear. You want this idea to spread like wildfire. People want to be like the boss—feel free to let them all have a similar focus on communicating with clarity. Don't ask "Am I making myself clear?"— that sounds like your dad scolding. Ask "Was that clear?" That leaves room for a request for clarification.

• *Walk the talk.* Simply put, match your words and actions. Model the values you espouse in your everyday deeds and actions. This is harder than it sounds, and when reduced to a cliché it loses its value. *Do what you say you'll do,* and make a concerted effort to live your word. When your integrity stands tall, it will raise the bar for everyone.

• *Don't take shortcuts.* Every organization wants to succeed. That's why, inevitably, there is a constant pressure to let the ends justify the means. This pressure becomes especially acute when either victory or failure is in immediate sight. That's when the usual ethical and moral constraints are abandoned—always for good reasons, and always "just this once"—in the name of expediency. Sometimes this strategy even works. But it sets the precedent for always using these tactics at critical moments—not to mention a kind of "mission creep" by which corner-cutting begins to invade operations even when they aren't at a critical crossroads.

- *Model absolute integrity. Integrity* is the word we use to describe the character of a person who is consistently principled and trustworthy—and above the temptation of lies, trickery, double-talk, shortcuts, and cover-ups. And every great leader I've ever known has always been described as someone of high integrity. You may not like them, or they may be take-no-prisoners competitors, but their word is their bond, they don't cheat or lie, the fight will be fair, and you won't be hearing of any scandals or transgressions at some point in the future.

Integrity is the bedrock of trustworthiness—the structural foundation that supports consistently honest, upstanding, fair behavior. Integrity is not always easy to see when present, but when it's missing, its absence glows like a neon sign. We have as evidence of this a virtual bonanza of recent tragic public integrity breaches so egregious that we now are hardly surprised when someone who previously built most of a powerful reputation on their upstanding citizenship subsequently falls from grace. Last names will suffice: Spitzer, Edwards, Woods, Madoff—the list goes on and on.

A Culture of Trust Is a Culture of Truth

As leaders, we are accountable for the success of the entity we lead. It can certainly be argued that success could be predicted by looking at the sum of the decisions we make as leaders. Our decisions create our outcomes. Access to factual, truthful information, undistorted by the organization, is essential to making solid decisions. If

the workspace is safe and if there is a *culture of truth*, you can justi-
fiably demand that people value the *integrity of the message*. If it is
not, they will naturally and automatically default to protecting the
safety of the messenger, and the message will get shaped accordingly.

In most organizations, we have access to incredible quantities
of data, facts, feedback, and other forms of information. Ideally, the
underlying truth or the integrity of that information is either certi-
fied as delivered or easy to confirm. However, on the political path
to the top of the organizational chart, information that is interpreted and communicated upward by people, as opposed to raw
data, usually gets classified into "good news" or "bad news" buckets.
And with regard to quality of information, the bottom line is, *information becomes unreliable at altitude*.

Good news flows easily within organizations—there will be lots
of messengers, and there will be full color coverage on every channel of the things we want to hear, with lots of people around to take
some of the credit. In contrast, information perceived as "bad"—
data that reveals goals missed, problems lurking, or feedback that
challenges or defeats our strategy—will be slower to form and travel
through the organization, more tempting to debate, and resistant to
conclusions, as we naturally want to position this data more positively than it appears. The line of volunteers to report these disappointments up the organizational chart will be short.

As leaders, we must turn this whole idea on its head. No more
buckets of only good and only bad. Instead, we must build a primary
and insatiable demand for the unvarnished facts, the raw data, the
actual measurements, the honest feedback, the real information.
Culturally, we must lead from the top, resisting the knee-jerk interpretations of everything we see and hear as "good news" or "bad
news," which immediately gives it more or less political currency or
value throughout the organization. We must value truth and speed
and acknowledge those who are courageous enough to carry those
risky messages. When we build a culture of judgment, we motivate
the bending of the truth, and we train the organization to hide or
deny things they know we have declared "bad" and amplify or
stretch things we have labeled "good."

We must instill a confidence and trust that leaders in the organization value the facts and the truth and the speed of delivery, not the judgments or interpretations of "good" or "bad," and that messengers are valued, not shot. If we can do this, then the entire behavior pattern of performance information flow will change for the better—and maybe dramatically. In the end, the truth must be dealt with and conveyed to your followers. A culture of truth saves time and money, and ultimately creates competitive advantage. This is extremely high leverage and noble work for leaders. Very few efforts will yield the payback associated with improving the speed and accuracy of the information you need most to make difficult or complex decisions. This opportunity exists only in a place made safe by leadership trustworthiness.

Supporting a culture of truth could be the most frustrating and difficult thing you will ever do as a leader. It takes real courage to come clean with your mistakes and failures; that's why I made authenticity—the courage to be yourself—the first step in this process. It takes real guts to be your real self and then admit your error to the world. But the habit of doing so makes you trustworthy, a man or woman of integrity—and that alone gives you the power to enforce a standard of integrity that will serve the organization in so many ways. When you can make mistakes and admit them, or put bad news out there and hold yourself accountable, you model this behavior for others.

One reason people within enterprises fear telling the truth to each other and to their bosses is that they know (consciously or unconsciously) the organization cannot properly distinguish between the message and the messenger. That's the main reason why leaders are often so insulated from the reality of what is going on around them: no one wants to be the human sacrifice for delivering the truth.

Bad News Doesn't Swim Upstream

There is a first cousin relationship between Chapters Two and Seven—that is, between *trust* and *communication*. Here is a story that shows the partnership of these two essential elements.

Tony, the CEO of large-cap public company, is a bright and sea-soned leader, and one of the smartest—and most authentic—things about him is his ability to identify and give full credit to the best things about the mentors that shaped his leadership philosophy on the way up.

For example, Tony readily admits that it was at Intel, working for Andy Grove, that he really learned about open, honest com-munication—including the loud, table-banging version called "constructive confrontation." By the same token, Tony said that at IBM he learned about building a culture that has respect for the individual. Finally, at several technology companies in the Valley Tony learned the Crosby Quality mantra—"Quality is free"—*design quality in, rather than test quality out.*

This story is about how Tony put those three street-smart lessons to use when he became a leader himself.

In early 1996, Tony took over as CEO of Data Management, Inc., a midsize software company with solutions for enterprise work-flow. At this time the company was preparing to release a major upgrade to its flagship software product. This was a very important maintenance fix—the company essentially promised its customers that all bugs were going to disappear and all features were going to work in this new version.

With so much at stake, and being the new chief on the scene, Tony understandably polled the top managers to make sure all of these promises could be delivered upon. He was told not to worry, that the product and the company were "in good shape." But something seemed wrong to Tony—his intuition was screaming *problem.* And in his walking around the company talking to workers, as was Tony's style, he began to hear rumblings that all of the optimism over this software release was overblown. Keying off his background—constructive confrontation, design quality-in, and concern for the individual—Tony continued digging for a few more clues to form his own opinion.

It soon became clear that the individual contributors in engi-neering and their management team had entirely different positions on the readiness of this software to ship to their customer base. Tony's mind reeled: he had been just a few weeks at the company, and now he had his first major crisis staring him in the face. He smelled a cover-up—a conspiracy of some scale—brewing in the hallways.

The normal reaction would have been to get mad and raise hell—something was wrong here, somebody was lying, and someone was in trouble. But as a leader, Tony decided to take a different tack: this was a moment, he realized, to establish a few important values in the culture of this company. Perhaps it was time to get angry—but with a specific purpose to that emotion. Tony's instinct was that this could be an event that created a painful but useful lesson in the company's history. A high road approach was the right strategy—and Tony knew that plan was much better than merely punishing his lieutenants and then allowing the organization to return to the status quo.

So Tony called a meeting, attended by every party involved in the process, both rank-and-file and top management. Once they had gathered, Tony made an opening statement to the effect that he thought it curious, and disturbing, that what he was hearing from the front line wasn't what he was hearing from senior management. He also stated, very clearly and calmly, that what he was interested in at this moment was the truth—the facts of the situation from everyone and anyone close enough to know. He then polled each person in the room to give their opinion about the state of the project—and got a very uncomfortable silence in response. But by just listening and not talking any further, little by little, piece by piece, the truth began to emerge. Tony then asked clarifying questions: What should we do about it? What have we told the customers? What's the status of the beta? He stayed very focused and professional, allowing the truth to find its way to the surface.

Eventually, all of the problems with the new product emerged. Tony then thanked everyone for their help and participation—and asked them all to leave. All, that is, except his direct reports.

Once they were alone, Tony told his lieutenants that this was the last meeting like this they would ever have. He told them,

"There is a one strike rule around here on matters of truth telling. And this was your one chance for the front line of the company to know the truth—and you guys are full of shit. This is not the way we do things around here anymore—and this is the last time you will make this mistake under my watch."

Implicit in Tony's message was that he distinguished between the obligations of the leaders in the organization and the obligations of the individual contributors. He wanted them to know that he held his leadership team to a higher standard—one which put the truth ahead of mollifying the boss. He challenged them to remove the blockage in the culture that had obviously created a danger in moving the truth—even if the facts were unfortunate—up the management chain. He was saying to them: either you are getting accurate information and you don't want to share it with me, or you're not even getting the right information—and both are unacceptable, just in different ways. In actuality, Tony was designing quality into the organization and teaching constructive confrontation by example.

Tony also told them: If I were to dismiss anyone here, it would violate the very rule I want to instill in you—that bad news must flow unobstructed, safely, upstream. But now you know the consequences of hiding the truth either from me or from yourselves. The next time will be very different.

The team left the room with each person confirming they heard and understood this distinction, and this message, and the consequences, very clearly.

You'll probably not be surprised to learn that this meeting became legend at the company. In part because from that moment on, everyone at the company knew that Tony's behavior not only matched his words but also confirmed his values.

A Culture of Trust Is a Culture of Innovation

Innovation flows from experimentation—indeed, it requires it—and experimentation inherently includes risk. Risk is required for reward. High-risk, low-cost environments (by "low-cost" I mean that the inevitable mistakes are not costly) are often fertile ground for real innovation breakthroughs that require the taking of some chances to create something meaningful. Safety is the bedrock of risk-taking. Trust is the basis of safety. Create trust, and you'll create a safe place to take risks; from there, all candidate ideas can be vetted, with no heightened concern about failure. The classic question "What would you do if you knew you couldn't fail?" actually needs an update. The more technically accurate way to put this is "What would you do if there were no *consequences* for failure?" It isn't failure that bothers us; it is the consequences for failure we imagine, whether real or perceived.

Most of you now own a digital camera, and you need look no further to see the direct relationship between willingness to take risk and the perceived "cost" of failure. There is no expense associated with a flawed digital photograph—financial or otherwise. You just hit the Delete button, and it disappears. No wasted film, slides, or prints. And we are aware of this relationship between mistakes and consequences when we pick up the camera—so we click away, taking many more photos digitally than we would have in a world of costly film. Because we know failure is free, we take chances, and in that effort we often get that one amazing picture that we wouldn't have if we were paying for all the mistakes.

Many golfers struggle to take their "range game" to the first tee of the golf course for the very same reason. On the driving range, there is no consequence for a shot that misses the target or even careens into the woods—it is just one practice ball in a bucket of a hundred, and no one is watching, and no one cares. There is no self-esteem at risk. The informative—and frustrating—aspect of this situation is that often this is when athletes find their best performance, when they can let go of all the fear-based tension that gets in the way of creativity and talent. Think about how fun it was the *second* time you rode a roller coaster or jumped off a rock into a lake—after you realized you wouldn't get hurt or die.

Paradoxically, perhaps, a sense of safety often drives greater risk-taking. Why? Because underpinning a lot of the assumption of risk is a calculation of the perceived (real or not) consequences of failure. Take away much of the anticipated pain of failure, and your followers will naturally take more chances. That, in turn, means that safety also drives *innovation*. The talents of creative and entrepreneurial people are less likely to flower in a low-trust, high-penalty environment. On the contrary, they are more likely to become risk-averse—and because innovation is the heart of continuing competitiveness, a lack of a sense of safety in the long run undermines the organization.

One of the stupidest things an organization can do is to punish a "good failure"—yet this happens all the time. A "good failure" is a term we use in Silicon Valley to describe a new business start-up or mature company initiative that, by most measures, is well-planned, well-run, and well-organized—yet for reasons beyond its control (an unexpected competitive product, a change in the market or economy) it fails.

Smart venture capitalists in the Valley long ago learned to distinguish the "good failures" (playing well, but still losing) from "bad failures" (playing badly and losing) and, trickiest of all, "bad successes" (playing badly but luckily winning, or simply being in the right place at the right time but believing you were responsible—never confuse luck with brains). This whole taxonomy explains why, in a move often inexplicable to outsiders, an entrepreneur from a failed start-up can find funding for his or her next venture, whereas one from a successful project outcome cannot.

Maverick at the Top. Apple Inc.'s cofounder and chairman Steve Jobs is a brilliant and complex man. There is no shortage of stories and legends about Jobs' mercurial behavior, his bizarre combination of warmth and cruelty, and his volatile ego. Yet for all of his personal unpredictability, when it comes to being an executive who drives innovation, Jobs is the most trustworthy of leaders. In fact, so deep is his integrity in dealing with his employees that I think history will recognize Apple as the most creative and innovative corporation of the first decade of the twenty-first century.

Of course, the company's incredible run of milestone products—the iMac, iPod, iPhone, iTunes, iPad—has been made possible in part because Apple has attracted some of the best designers in the high-tech industry. But far more important is the work environment that Jobs has created for these talented people. At the heart of this culture is what is, for the business world, an almost unprecedented acceptance of failure. Not only is employee risk-taking encouraged, but risk avoidance is actually punished. Employees who don't think big, who don't swing for the fences (as captured in the company catch phrase that has entered everyday language: "insanely great") ultimately find themselves marginalized at Apple, if not driven out. Steve pushes the envelope with ferocity—he abhors conservative fly-with-the-flock thinking. He knows that it takes outrageous thinking to create outrageously great products.

Unlike every competitor of the company—and indeed, almost every other company in the world—Apple has a leader who is a bigger maverick than any of the people who work for him. In the case of the iPod and iTunes, Jobs even changed Apple's entire business model in pursuit of what he accurately concluded to be a huge new market opportunity. This kind of behavior creates the most high-trust, low-penalty work environment imaginable—and the innovation just flows. As the leader of an innovative enterprise, Jobs has no current peers.

A Culture of Trust Is a Culture of Performance

Similar to the challenge of differentiating between the message and the messenger, we must learn to differentiate between the quality of the work—that is, performance—and the quality of the worker—that is, integrity. Too often we allow ourselves to see a mistake or failure on the field as a reason to start distrusting the person running the play. When someone's work or performance disappoints us, we have a tendency—a dangerous one—to doubt or distrust *them*, sometimes without realizing this is misplaced logic. And when we do this, we signal to the team that performance is linked to personal trust—when you fall short on a goal or objective, you may find yourself losing the faith of the team. Yet we know this is wrong. We develop a trust or distrust for someone's work, which is a performance issue—not the same as trust or distrust of the person behind the job, which is a matter of integrity.

What this means in practice is that you should never punish a good person for delivering bad news—or even, on occasion, bad work. One big mistake that both leaders and followers make regarding trustworthiness is conflating it with performance. This is a very destructive pattern of behavior—and it costs a lot of organizations some of their best talent. When the clarity of this distinction is lost, that feeling of safety evaporates, and the risk-taking behavior once characteristic of high-trust environments disappears with it. Performance problems should be managed fairly and with little judgment of the person's underlying character, *unless* that is the issue at the root of the trouble. Ultimately, improving performance is often merely a matter of feedback, course correction, and some coaching.

By the same token, major breaches of trust and integrity must be punished swiftly—making the punishment as public an object lesson as possible. As a leader, you are not going to "fix" a thief, a pathological liar, or a professional con artist—all of these must go, immediately. The cost of untruths to an organization can be huge in terms of time, money, trust, and reputation. You cannot take the risk of offering a second chance. In my coaching practice, there are three failure modes that I will decline to coach—integrity, commitment, and chronic selfishness (that is, manipulating outcomes for individual gain at the expense of the larger opportunity)—because these are character traits, not matters of skill, practice, knowledge, or experience.

In my experience, great leaders are always conscious that they are creating institutional myths and legends, so they will often seek out an example of an employee who failed nobly, or who delivered bad news for the right reasons, and will publicly honor that behavior. Doing that just once—and thus removing the fear of "shooting the messenger"—can have an extraordinarily powerful tonic effect upon the rank-and-file.

Trustworthiness, like authenticity before it and all of the steps after it, is never entirely pure. We are fallible human beings, after all. Each of us will occasionally betray our family, friends, and, as leaders, our followers, to some degree. Everyone fails to achieve perfection. So the goal for a leader is to make those wrong choices as rarely as possible; admit them quickly, completely, and with humility; fix them as quickly as you can; and make full recompense when you cannot.

What you should *never* do when you have compromised your trustworthiness is to indulge in denial or cover-up. Denial blocks the path back to truth, which means that the damage to one's trustworthiness and credibility is never healed. As for covering up a crime: if the last twenty years of Washington scandals has taught us anything, it is this: "It is never the crime, it is the cover-up." Cover-ups make everything worse—right, Tiger Woods? Right, Bill Clinton? Cover-ups are particularly expensive and destructive to organizations built on trust—they waste time and money, and they create another set of deceptions—and concerns about trustworthiness—that will eventually have to be untangled and defused.

Take Your Pain Quickly and Acutely—and Move On

If the world of high-profile, public breaches of integrity has proven anything, it is that the cover-up is almost always worse than the crime. Yet leaders and public figures of many varieties never seem to learn this. Here's one such story from the world of normal people in a normal setting. This disease is not limited to Wall Street, Washington, or professional sports.

There was a lab manager for a medical device company I worked with in the early '90s. He ran a remote site staffed by a very talented group of researchers. He seemed to be a good boss and able to handle the fact that his technical expertise was probably not as great as that of the people working for him.

This lab was doing very technical, very precise experiments dealing with large samples of titanium replacement hip and knee joints. The statistical computations were particularly complex.

Right in the middle of this research, some of the results began to look very suspect. When the lab manager was told there might be a problem, he investigated—only to find that the problem had indeed been caused by sloppy procedures in the lab. That is, it was ultimately his responsibility.

The next decision was the beginning of the real problems. The lab manager decided *not* to take the news to his boss, the CEO. Instead, he chose to hide and mask the problem with the data—and when it leaked out, as these things always do, the lab manager dodged questions, danced around the topic, and worst of all, altered the data to make it look a bit less troubling.

Keep in mind, we're not talking about toaster manufacturing here, but sophisticated medical experiments on which lives might depend. Eventually, the news, as doctored by the lab manager, reached the CEO, a major industry figure whose reputation for honesty and technical precision was beyond reproach. Once the CEO saw the data, he knew part of it was fraudulent. It just didn't make sense.

But, being a decent man and a good leader, the CEO decided to give his lab manager one chance to tell him the truth. Instead of coming down hard on the manager, the CEO waited a day for him to call and confess and explain his role in the situation. When the phone didn't ring that day, or the next, the CEO approached the manager and asked for an explanation. The manager's reply was partially accurate, but wholly insufficient to explain the discrepancies.

Why did you take so long to tell me this? the CEO demanded. The lab manager responded with a desperate song-and-dance to rationalize his actions—why he didn't report the problem sooner and what went wrong in the first place—both stories that the CEO knew not to be true.

Unable to take any more, the CEO cut his losses and informed this manager that he was no longer employed at the company. He knew he could never trust the man again.

Now, here's the irony. Once the smoke cleared, and the CEO dug deeper into the story, it became apparent that what had gone wrong in the lab was actually not terribly serious—the results were not tremendously far off from what would have been expected—and there had likely been a series of simple, honest mistakes that could explain the discrepancy. All that the lab manager had needed to do was to quickly report the problem to headquarters and ask for its support in launching an investigation.

But even after the lab manager had covered up the problem data, when the CEO gave him one last chance he could have made a full confession, admitted that he had hidden the bad news because he was scared, and asked for help—all of which might have momentarily stalled his career but ultimately raised his reputation for honesty in the CEO's eyes.

Instead, the lab manager had failed himself, his people, and his company. Most of all, he failed the one character test his job required him to pass.

As for the CEO, coming out of this mess he asked himself the two necessary questions. First, is there something in our organizational culture that reinforces this type of lying behavior? After much study, the CEO concluded *no, because we have had other, comparable situations in which employees have told the truth.* And second, is there something wrong with our HR processes that we would hire and promote into a position of responsibility someone with these ethics? This one was much tougher to answer—indeed, the CEO was never again really sure. At best, he could only conclude that sometimes you don't really know the character of a person until their mettle is tested in the crucible of a stressful situation. He also concluded what I have just been saying—it's usually not the crime, but the cover-up that causes all the pain.

Put simply: You must separate performance from behavior. Punish breaches of trust; reward good failures. And protect your own trustworthiness and integrity at all costs.

As leaders, our goal—in fact, our obligation—must be to do what it takes to create a high-trust communications environment.

It is tedious, never-ending work, but it is worth the rewards. One of the first and very best markers of an environment where legitimate trust is present is the quality and speed of the flow of information, both structured and casual—bad news, good news, up the org, down the org, sideways, all ways. Analyzing the way that information moves—which is the juice from which decisions are made in an organization—is your first and likely most useful set of clues as to where there is trust and where there is fear. Sometimes the info stops with one specific person who doesn't pass it onward—or who manipulates or spins it to suit their needs. Or it gets derailed just before it gets to another specific person, for fear of their treatment of the message—or, more dangerously, treatment of the messenger. Or sometimes departments or topics have a profile of their risk aversion that shows up in the way information behaves around them. Developing a keen eye for the pattern of casual and sub-rosa information flow will give you great insight to who your truth tellers are, and who is either a perpetrator or a victim of fear in your workplace.

A working environment of trust is a place where our teams stay focused, give their utmost effort, and in the end do their best work—that is, a place when we can trust ourselves, trust others, trust our surroundings, or—best of all—trust all three.

The Essentials of Being Trustworthy

- You won't be trusted because you are the boss—in fact, that makes it harder. Assume a distrust of power. Work through it. You must go first—be trustworthy, and others will trust you. Your trustworthiness is a model for the organization.

- Trust is about safety. It is fragile. It takes time to build, and it can be ruined in a flash. You will not create trust with authority.

- Trust is essential to the quality—and speed—of all kinds of information. This is the essential business reason to insist on trust-building behaviors. Leading a high-performance organization with low trust is almost impossible.

- Innovation is about the perceived consequence of risk. Try to make the cost of an honest mistake as rational, and minimal, as possible. You want people swinging for the fence.

- Stand on integrity to create safety. You will be rewarded with risk-taking, innovation, and commitment.

- There is nothing more precious to your leadership credibility than integrity.

CHAPTER THREE

BEING COMPELLING
The Commitment to Winning

The task of the leader is to get his people from
where they are to where they have not been.

—*Henry Kissinger*

In the compelling zest of high adventure and of
victory, and in creative action, that man finds his
supreme joys.

—*Antoine de Saint-Exupéry*

As my colleague Barry Posner, former dean of the Leavy School of
Business at Santa Clara University, reminds us in *The Leadership
Challenge*, the qualities we want in a leader are essentially the same
ones we want in a friend or coworker or a partner—*except for one*.
In leaders, we also need to see an additional attribute—we need to
know their *vision* if we are to enroll in their cause. Leaders must
imagine and articulate a compelling future that enrolls others. This
is where the train stops, and you should exit if you realize that
leadership is not for you.

Authenticity and trustworthiness create the basis for productive
and committed relationships. People who are authentic and trustworthy are usually good and fair. They aren't likely to lie to you or

screw you over, and you'll likely feel like you really know who they are. They might be candidates for a good friendship. But it is not obvious that we should follow them—anywhere. These first two virtues are necessary but insufficient to create committed follower-ship. Above all else, the thing that defines leaders is that they have not just friends or admirers—they have followers.

To be willing to act of our own free will and choose to follow someone, we must experience something distinctly different, some-thing more than the feeling of being "inspired" or "safe"—we must feel *compelled*. Almost any version of success requires committed *action* toward goals. And action requires teams of people assembled around leaders aligned with a shared, bold vision. Compelling leaders create a following that is different from one of "believers" (those are for gospel preachers and spiritual teachers); leaders find and inspire followers who commit not just with their mind or hearts, but also with their time and energy.

We followers are compelled by a cause. This starts with a vision that expresses a substantial commitment in tangible ways. Leaders must paint a picture for those they wish to enroll—a vision of what winning will look like and how participants can contribute their talents in the pursuit of that vision and share in the ultimate success. From the perspective of those who follow, the message is "This vision has a place for you, and I want you involved in this project." If you ever doubt the power of a cause—consider Lance Armstrong's massive success with Livestrong. There are dozens of worthy and compelling campaigns and programs to raise money for cancer research—great organizations like the Susan Komen Race for the Cure, The V Foundation, and others. But there is nothing to equal Livestrong for enrolling ordinary people in a big vision—and it's all about that crazy idea that bonds people together around the *cause*—the *yellow rubber bracelet*. To wear one says to everyone that you have joined the club, for $2 or $2 million, or for nothing given except your emotional and public commitment to the vision Lance has communicated for ending cancer, having gone through the experience of having cancer himself. The brilliance in the symbolism of the wristbands is well known and has been copied by hundreds of other causes as a surefire way to publicly show who has signed up for each campaign—and these bracelets, of all colors and styles now, serve as great conversation starters. They allow people to feel the pride of having signed on to a team that others respect. I was walking down Fifth Avenue in New York a few years ago and noticed (it was hard not to) the number of guys in $3,000 suits— and yellow rubber wristbands. Since that moment I have never, ever been confused about the inherent and enduring willingness of human beings to be enrolled. They are just waiting for a cause that speaks to their values and, at the same time, to something bigger than themselves. This reminds me of something my father told me: "There is no such thing as bad weather, only inadequate clothing." In this case, it would be slightly different—*there is no such thing as an unwilling follower, only one who has not yet seen a compelling reason to join*. It is our job to create that reason, in them, to step onto the field and play.

We are compelled by leaders. By the same token, no one will sacrifice for a project, no matter how exciting, if the leader hasn't made a full and clear—and public—commitment. That commitment must inspire others to make their own choice to join and dedicate themselves to the mission at hand. Unusually Excellent leaders sustain authenticity with personal courage and are trustworthy to others over time with an unshakable integrity. The best leaders are compelling to others because they have a deep and burning commitment that they can articulate and share in a way that makes others want to be part of that idea—that motivates others to see themselves as members of that club. Whether it is a big global idea like cataloging all the world's information at Google, or having the finest restaurant in your neighborhood, it matters only that you can paint this picture in a powerful way and articulate a place in that vision for others to contribute. Finally, great leaders compel us with these ideas because they are engaged—right in the middle of the action, not at arm's length. It is clear they will sweat and toil with the team, be the last one to leave, and sacrifice more than they expect from anyone.

We are compelled by "team." I don't know anyone itching to be managed, but I also don't know anyone unwilling to be *led*. Each of us wants to be part of something real and something meaningful; not to be part of a plan, but to join a *cause*—something bigger than us—a joint effort that speaks to our own sense of possibility and opportunity. Great leaders evoke the emotion and energy of being involved in a crusade. They give people a chance to be emotional co-owners of an exciting future that they can have a hand in creating and shaping. We don't want to be merely an employee; we want to be part of a *team*, working together to create something important. Often, the highest loyalty we'll ever know is to our *team*— beyond the mission, bigger than the goal, and sometimes deeper than our loyalty to ourselves.

It may be a cliché, but it is true nonetheless, that "great followers make great leaders." They know what it takes. And that means that great leadership is not about convincing your followers to act; rather, it's about creating the setting in which they compel *themselves* to accomplish great things. Most leaders I know want to guide or steer or coach, not push or pull or coerce—the energy must come from an inspired team, compelled to act.

If indeed, as many believe, the job of leaders is to inspire their teams to create and own the future, then it follows that a leader's vision of that future—and a big, bold commitment to it—is what compels others to join that crusade.

Choice and Obligation

You have to *earn* your followers at the outset of your company, organization, or project, and you must *value* them every day of its duration, in subtle or explicit ways, be it for a week or for twenty years. Otherwise, at best they will give you suboptimal performance, and at worst, they will leave you. Not valuing employees is exhibit A in the definition of "being taken for granted." They are so often forgotten and expected to just keep putting out, because, after all, you are paying them a fair wage, right? If instead you keep reminding yourself that the best and brightest are with you for now, but they always have options, you'll grasp the concept that will keep you grounded on this journey: *No one is obliged to follow you.* When you are willing to accept this statement as fact, you can ask yourself the ultimate leadership question: *Why would your best and brightest be willing to be led by you?*

Can you answer that question not from *your* point of view but from theirs? In my experience many successful and veteran leaders cannot. Instead, they have relied on some combination of authority and organizational power, charisma, luck, and years of trial and error, and some good mentorship to teach them how to get people to follow. It may be that they have never led from influence, but only from power, and thus they have never thought about this idea. You too may decide to follow that path and "feel" your way to leadership success. But the odds are long against your getting there.

The notion that you must earn your followers' loyalty certainly competes with the inherent authority of your job, but Unusually Excellent leaders realize that there is a mind-set they can adopt that keeps them focused on the essentials of credibility. Your best, most talented, and most valuable followers are really volunteers, and because of those very attributes they are often in considerable demand elsewhere. What that means, whether you know it or not, is that these value creators—your best and brightest (rainmakers)—are constantly in demand in the world. They have options. Your competitors would love to have them. This also means that the best of your team won't tolerate sub-par leadership—they don't need to. The good news is that the culture they demand, and the standard they set for others as they raise the bar, are both incredibly healthy side effects of their presence—and things you cannot create without them on your team.

Attracting the Best and Brightest

How do you attract and retain your best followers? In short, by making the experience of being part of your crusade more compelling and emotionally rewarding than any other alternative. And also by appreciating, in private and public ways, the contributions they make to the success of the organization. And how do you do that? Well, you've already taken the first two steps by being both authentic and trustworthy. As we've already said, that reduces the fear and confusion level in the work environment, which frees the people following you to be more audacious and creative. That is a great start, and it pays dividends broadly.

However, perhaps the best approach to retaining your A Players is to learn, as early as possible in your career as a leader, how to answer the question posed earlier (*Why would your best and brightest be willing to be led by you?*) with a real strategy. Let me give you some guideposts, based on thirty years of studying leaders: the *five E's* that will help you ensure the followership you want and need in order to compete and win.

1. *Great leaders know how to engage*. Engagement is about getting our attention—in the same way that a great advertisement has stopping power, a leader can capture our imagination and hold our focus. Engagement is about being interesting—but more important, interested—that is, interested in people. It is amazing how many times I've heard people describe someone as "engaging," and I know that the person they refer to is primarily a great listener who knows how to take a sincere interest in other people. There are few things as flattering as someone who seems to genuinely care about who we are, and seek to know something about us beyond our name or job title or what we can do for them. Sometimes we say more by talking less. Engagement is a practice—although it comes more naturally or easily for some, all leaders can learn to engage in ways that connect them with the people they want to know and need to influence. There is no excuse for engaging poorly, and it will stop your leadership effectiveness cold. It all starts here.

2. *Great leaders enroll people*. All great leaders are great salespeople—this is so essential to enrollment that if you don't like to "sell" you should think long and hard about being a leader. *Selling* is not a bad word, and you should be wary of any discomfort this causes

you—it will hamper your results. You are always selling, even if you don't want to use that word. Ideas, proposals, recruiting top talent, your own leadership credibility, points of view, the vision, the mission, the plan—all require your ability to persuade others in a forthright and transparent way. Selling is the process of meeting needs with solutions. And great leaders know it is never enough to just make the pitch; they also need to close the deal. They know how to sign us up for their cause. They know how to ask for the order. One of the main reasons some founders and entrepreneurs don't scale into real leaders is that, whatever deal may be in front of them, they simply cannot close it. Lieutenant Colonel William Travis famously drew a line in the sand at the Alamo and asked his volunteers to step over it. The act of enrollment is the act of public commitment, an implied contract that can be broken by the follower only at the cost of shame, and by the leader only at the cost of betrayal. But remember, enrollment is possible only if you have engaged in a compelling way.

3. With the team in place, the next—and arguably the most important—*task of the leader is to energize the troops*, to forge them into a cohesive unit, orient them toward the common goal, and marshal the resources to support them in their task. What energizes a workforce most—and most naturally—is the passion of the leader. Like trust, leaders create energy by modeling it—by talking and moving through the organization with a sense of purpose, conviction, and urgency. Low-energy leaders lead low-energy organizations, and that may not be a predictor of failure, but I'd bet on the woman who gets her team *moving with enthusiasm* toward the end zone. We'll look more at the energizing process, from the followers' perspective, in the next section. Low energy signals no real enrollment. Stop. Go back to step #2.

4. The fourth—and certainly not the least—challenge for the leader is *to empower his or her followers* to assume the responsibility of being leaders as well—if not of others as supervisors, then over themselves and their careers. Followers for whom empowerment feels real—not merely a concept—believe they really *own* something. Ownership has been transferred. It is their baby—they aren't

doing someone else's work or managing someone else's project. They have stopped renting a room—they have bought the house. Now they act like owners, not renters—they'll fix that leaky faucet or squeaky door instead of calling the landlord to complain. But unfortunately, everyone knows that the leader who cannot delegate and tries to do everything himself is likely to attract only helpers, not real partners, and is ultimately destined to fail. Yet this happens thousands of times each day. These are the people we call "control freaks," and you may have just such a boss right now—or you may even be one.

Why, if there are endless examples of why aggrandizing complete control is a disaster, do so many leaders still insist upon doing so? The answer, I think, is a complex dynamic of *ego and fear*. *Ego*, because some leaders believe that, by dint of their having achieved their current exalted position, only they are sufficiently competent to do the task at hand, so why should they wait for their subordinates to screw things up? Why not just do the job themselves? Thus, ironically, these leaders prove that they are undeserving of the jobs for which they alone are qualified, because this dysfunction will ultimately catch up with them and become their Achilles heel.

Fear, because these leaders are more terrified by the prospect of failure than drawn to the potential for success. This insecurity drives them to gather up more and more control over operations in order to have complete control over their destiny. This too is ironic, because in regaining control over details, they inevitably lose control over the big picture—and their greatest fear, failure, becomes true.

5. The fifth *E* is more subtle and subjective: *enthusiasm*. Great leaders are compelling in large part because they have found the way to make their mission exciting to followers. To be truly compelling requires a leader to be both inspiring and relevant. The inspiration comes from the leader's boldness and vision. The relevance comes from the potential follower's personal calculation that the leader has the proven competence needed for the task and that he or she has established a win-win proposition for both himself or herself and for

the potential follower. The familiar, essential question, "WIFM?"— What's in it for me?—must be answered by all followers.

Thus the great leader's message is not just "Follow me" but also "Connect with me. I know what to do. Together we will accomplish something great that you will look back on with pride."

Notice that, once again, this appeal rests on both authenticity and trustworthiness. The kind of people you want on your team, the kind you expect to give their all to the cause, are going to be studying you very carefully to see whether you are sincere in your call for them to follow—and that you are as passionate and committed as you expect them to be. They want to be sure that they are entering an environment that will be safe enough for them to do their best. If they are going to invest in the future you see, they expect you to invest in them.

Keeping Your Best on Board

Now, what attributes constitute a compelling place to work and learn in, beyond one that has an inspiring vision, a big commitment, and a way for everyone to contribute? What keeps that place that was so great at the beginning just as great over time—for years and years? It is one thing to attract great people, but it is another one to retain them and create a consistently compelling experience long after the shine of the newness has faded. The best and brightest will tell you, if you ask them, that they require two basic qualities of their workplace in order to be happy, long term—and if these two conditions are present, they will probably stay with you as long as you stay with them in making these things right. These are *honest communication* and *meaningful challenge*.

Cheerleader

Here is a story about enrollment and reenrollment.

Acme was an Internet security company that enjoyed excellent growth from its founding in 2000 to its sale in 2005 to a major technology company for close to a billion dollars. Its CEO, Andy, was one of the most compelling human beings I've ever had the pleasure to work with. He was absolutely 100-percent comfortable in selling the cause, the vision, and the mission of his company. His passion and ability to paint a picture of how Acme was going to change the world were infectious. You could just feel yourself looking for a way to get involved every time he spoke about this company.

Andy also understood something incredibly important: *to keep your employees engaged, you must regularly re-create the original passion, simulating the reasons they first joined the team.* That means it is not enough to be sufficiently compelling to get great people to join the organization. He believed he couldn't just recruit great people and then forget about them. He had to keep reminding them, in fun and creative ways, of the experience they had when they signed up—to give them ways to feel the excitement they felt when they joined, all over again. He wondered: *why would you do this for new recruits but not find a way to create the same experience for the team wearing your jerseys?*

For several years it seemed that the company tended to introduce new platforms or major updates of its products at roughly six-month intervals. This was partially by design, but more so by pure coincidence of the product strategy and competitive marketplace. And the company would gear up for each of these introductions with a publicity kit, sales training curricula, press tour, marketing materials, and so on. The team put a lot of effort into these introductions, and each was definitely an "all hands on deck" time in the company.

For most companies this would have been more than enough. But Andy, being an Unusually Excellent leader, saw an opportunity beyond the product. He realized that these regular events were a perfect opportunity to reenroll and reenergize his team. So at every new product event the senior team created homemade motivational videos, handed out T-shirts, and took the opportunity to remind the entire team about the vision and mission of Acme—and how fun it is to change the world. Andy understood that even the best people's emotional fuel tanks eventually get low—that although they might remember that moment two years ago when they sat with him in Starbucks and he sold them on the crazy vision of Acme to become a big, important, leadership company, now they were tired.

That's why Andy decided that the real target of each new product introduction was not the company's customers—they'd get the message through the now reliable processes of external marketing and sales—but rather the employees of the company. This was the moment to recommit them and reengage them to a vision of an even bigger, better, cooler, neater, more ass-kicking company than the one they had originally signed up for.

Looking at some of those videos now can be amusing—they are frenetic pep rallies about how great Acme is, the great people that have gathered there, and how it will dust the competition—but they did the job. As I was writing this, I decided to call Andy and ask him to explain in greater depth his strategy at the time. What he told me was, "I had to keep reminding people why they wanted to come to Acme every day." He added that it began when he asked himself: *Why is the company doing all of this cheerleading for its customers and media—and not doing it for its own people? Why do we have a press tour and not an employee tour?*

Finally, Andy realized that what he wanted was to create the equivalent for his employees of being recruited to Acme for the first time. "I wanted to sign everyone up for a new 'emotional' contract with the company." And it worked incredibly well. Turnover was ultra-low, morale stayed high, and the company had a home-run outcome.

Born-Again Employees

Once you recognize the concept, you see it in all sorts of good companies. I work with a life sciences company run by a guy named Dan. The company is working on some extremely exciting personalized medicine products for cancer treatment.

Needless to say, this is a very high-stakes business—you either succeed brilliantly or you fail completely. It's like horseshoes and hand grenades—close isn't good enough. The work itself is noble, and enormously meaningful and important, and serves as a huge natural motivator. Most people working there have drunk the Kool-Aid, so to speak, but there is an ever-present fear of imminent disaster.

I've consistently reminded Dan that, as a leader, you need to always remember that the ideas that seem most obvious are often the least communicated messages. As CEO, you have all of the relevant data at your fingertips—but the further down you go in the organization, the thinner that information becomes. So what you casually assume *everybody* knows may, in fact, be known only by you. By the same token, just because you are enthusiastic about the company, the vision, and the future (because you have great information and all the necessary context at your fingertips) doesn't mean everyone in the organization shares that enthusiasm; they may need to know some of what you know, or perhaps the perspective that is obvious to you, to feel like you do.

This means that if you want to be compelling with your team, you should assume *nothing*. Take nothing for granted. Each day is a new day. Just because you talked about how exciting this company is at the last all-hands meeting doesn't mean the message has stuck—or is even remembered. So I tell Dan, every time you get in front of your company I want you to speak your personal commitment to the mission again like it is brand-new—to tell them why *you're* so excited to get in your car each morning to come to work. Give people a new or refreshed reason to follow you. They want to feel your commitment again; they want to clip into your vision like they did before. If they need a reminder, this will do the trick. If this doesn't work, then you need a different tune-up. This is one of those "needs" that no one will ever ask for directly but that everyone wants. It is a leader's job to supply this nutrient before the signs of neglect appear.

Enthusiasm is a renewable resource. Part of being compelling is reminding yourself that people want and need to be reenrolled all the time. This message doesn't have to be over the top to be compelling. It may entail just reminding your team, once per quarter, why you come to the office every day, and letting them reflect on the reason they do the same.

In Dan's case, the message in his heart is: *I come to his company each morning because, when I'm seventy years old, I want to be able to look back and know that we were the company that history says found the cure for leukemia—that would be something I'd be very proud of being a part of. And that's going to make me really happy. I want to be part of that kind of change in the world, and I think you guys want to be too. I know I've said that to you for the last ten quarters, but I still believe it. And I believe it even more than I believed it yesterday.*

Is that presentation a bit theatrical? Sure, but it is also honest and sincere—and compelling. So he should share it. There is lots of upside and almost no downside. Don't take for granted that once enrolled is always enrolled. We need to remind our teams of the reason they joined us once upon a time—and we need to do that more often than we may think.

Tell Me the Truth

It is tempting for leaders to communicate only what seems positive or exciting or motivating—and this points them toward presenting only "good news." The top contributors don't want to hear just good news. They want the truth. They can handle the truth, and being treated with the respect of the truth is more important, by a mile, than having the data scrubbed for fear that it might scare or discourage the troops. If you think your subordinates can't handle bad news, you may have hired the wrong people or underestimated the ones you have. If you can take it, so can they. In fact, you will find that the best people actually find reality, even if it is bad news, compelling. They love a challenge—that's why you wanted them in the first place—and they appreciate the truth.

Jim Collins, in his classic book *Good to Great* (Harper, 2001), coined the term "Stockdale Paradox" to describe the behavior of a team unified around a long-term goal when faced with nearly intractable short-term obstacles. The term derives from a quote by

Admiral James Stockdale, who survived seven years as a North Vietnamese POW (and earned the Medal of Honor). Collins quotes Stockdale as saying "This is a very important lesson: You must never confuse faith that you will prevail in the end—which you can never afford to lose—with the discipline to confront the most brutal facts of your current reality, whatever they might be."

Collins goes on to say that in his own research, this same paradox—that of the team growing both more optimistic, and yet at the same time more pragmatic, when faced with greater challenges and near-term failures—as long as they can still believe in the validity of the overall vision. Collins writes: "In every case, the management team responded with a powerful psychological duality. On the one hand, they stoically accepted the brutal facts of reality. On the other hand, they maintained an unwavering faith in the endgame, and a commitment to prevail as a great company despite the brutal facts."

The history of sports is filled with stories that exemplify the Stockdale Paradox. Think of teams such as the 2004 Boston Red Sox, down 0–3 in the American League Pennant Race against their eternal enemy, the New York Yankees—a predicament no team had survived in a century—yet somehow managing to find new reserves of competitiveness and go on to win the next four games and the series. Or the 1951 New York Giants, thirteen games out on August 12, embarking on a sixteen-game winning streak, taking thirty-seven of their last forty-four games—and then beating the Brooklyn Dodgers with Bobby Thompson's home run in the league play-off. The dire situations these teams faced were more than offset by their long-term belief that they would ultimately triumph.

Apple Computer's great comeback from its lost decade of 1989–1999 to its triumph in the new century was due to a corps of employees who still believed in the company's old magic—and responded quickly when Steve Jobs returned to lead them. There are similar stories to tell about Harley-Davidson, Ford Motor Company, and IBM. In case after case, great but troubled companies find their way back to glory because their employees never surrender, but only need a great leader to lead them out of their troubles. In fact, you can even make the case that all that these great leaders really do is empower these employees to execute the recovery strategy they already have in their minds—and have simply been waiting for someone in authority to listen to.

It goes even deeper than that. Research has found that most people will stay with a very tough situation—right up until the day they are lied to. After that, all bets are off. Their commitment is no longer worth it, and they will walk away. Note that this is exactly the moment when you, as leader, will be under the greatest pressure to dissemble, hide bad news, and fake optimism. Once again, you will see the importance of authenticity and trustworthiness as essential ingredients to the credibility you need in those moments. And you will realize why the truth, and the challenge it often presents, is irresistably compelling to the people on your team whom you value and want to keep the most.

Keep Me Challenged

Talented people want and need challenging work. It is not good news for them when their job gets easy—and boring. They want to take on the hard problems, the project that makes their idea better than every other product out there, the customer that no one else can tame, or the spreadsheet that no one else can decipher. For leaders, the other part of the retention equation is to stay in touch with and in tune with the nature of the work assigned to the people you value the most. It has to be meaningful—connected to the vision and important to the success of the mission—and it has to be challenging, such that it will push those high performers to struggle and learn in the course of getting things done. Take the time to just ask this group of folks what they love about their work; you'll find that virtually every answer you hear contains something about challenging assignments, work that matters, and knowing that their project is aligned with the most important goals the organization must accomplish. You'll never hear anything about making it easy. It's true that there are some people who are looking for an easy job, who will leave the company if they can't locate one within the organization. But the high achievers are looking for challenging assignments because they keep them learning, and they'll find one somewhere, even if they have to leave.

No Hard Feelings

There is one more *E*. And for this one we have to reverse our perspective; to look into the other end of the telescope, if you will. This *E* is *empathy*. I am convinced that it is impossible to be a great leader if you do not have a sophisticated understanding of what it means to be *your* follower.

Empathy is often challenging for leaders precisely because their natural aptitude has always made them poor followers or difficult followers or only very brief followers. They can't easily see what others might be seeing—or, more important, feel what others might be feeling. The old saw that you have to be a good follower to be a good leader sounds sensible, but you rarely see it in practice. There are many great leaders—think of Winston Churchill—who appear to have been absolutely *terrible* followers. Those traits that make you want to assert your vision onto reality are typically antithetical to the ones that make you want to serve somebody else's view of the future.

That said, it is very rare to encounter a great leader, especially in our modern, more democratic world, who does not have a deep respect for and understanding of his or her followers. To possess that necessary understanding, leaders must be able to stand in their followers' shoes and see themselves from that viewpoint. That takes us back to the question we asked earlier: *Why would anyone want to be led by you?*

We've already responded with the behavioral traits of leaders that would motivate followers. But there's more, some of it paradoxical.

Followers' Rights

We want our leaders to be authentic and human—just like us, only a little better. This is one of those great paradoxes of human society. We want the people who lead us to be flawed, unpredictable, and complicated like we are—that makes them human. It enables us to connect with them emotionally—a crucial part of the team-building process between leader and followers. Yet at the same time we expect our leaders to be nearly flawless, consistent, and transparent, so that we can safely entrust them with our fate. Fulfilling both of these desires is, obviously, impossible—yet another reason why great leadership is both difficult and rare.

We want our leaders to tell us a compelling story while at the same time being honest with us. Yet another paradox. By definition, a "vision" is a prediction of the future based on limited information in the present and dependent on a specific set of events occurring between now and then. That is to say, it is a fiction, with a small chance of ever becoming a reality.

Yet it is just such a vision, and a compelling one at that, that followers require in order to buy into a cause. And once they've made that emotional purchase, they expect the leader to be trustworthy enough to always be honest with them.

One last paradox: *We want to invest our leaders, and they have some authority over our lives, but we reserve the right as individuals to assert our own authority.* This one can be a minefield. Historically, this was much less of a problem for leaders: society already asserted its own class hierarchies (you may know of Wellington's remarks, apparently affectionate, that his soldiers were "the scum of the earth") into which followers self-selected for their proper roles, and leaders were often rewarded with some form of "divine right."

Obviously, that isn't quite the case in twenty-first-century global business. Indeed, most people who would be classified as "followers" don't consider themselves that at all: rather, they believe they are merely voluntarily assigning authority to someone else, and they can rescind that loan at any time. At the same time, most also believe that even as they are part of a larger organization or team, they nevertheless still retain full autonomy over their lives and careers.

Obviously, there are real disadvantages to this arrangement, especially when it comes to aligning the organization toward a single goal—or, during emergencies, managing by fiat rather than consensus. But it has huge advantages as well. For one thing, it is much easier to empower followers who want and expect to make their own decisions. It also makes it possible to create a "mass customized" work environment in which each worker creates a personal "safe" place for greatest productivity—a task that is nearly impossible when imposed from the top down.

We want to admire our leaders. This doesn't mean they have to be paragons of virtue, but we do expect them to be smart, brave, competent, and most of all, successful. If we admire a leader, and that leader presents us with a vision that is both inspiring and relevant, we literally can't help but follow them.

Finally, *we want our leaders to be committed to the cause.* I cannot overstress this. Being compelling requires passion. We want to follow people who are as passionate about the future as they have convinced us to be. Furthermore, we don't want this to be a temporary, fairweather passion that will evaporate when times get tough and leave us high and dry. We want the captain to be not just committed to piloting us to our destination, but also willing to go down with the ship if we hit an iceberg. We want our leaders to bet the farm to prove they've earned the right to lead us. Leaders must keep speaking their commitment and the possibility they see, long after they think we know it. They can't lose faith. They are merchants of hope. Even when the future looks bleak, leaders can't blink. If the leader balks, the team panics.

As leaders, we must be compelling. This is the on-ramp to the topic of Chapter Four, Leading People. There is no substitute for talent, and those with real talent are never looking for a job. They need to be recruited, and thus they must be compelled to join. To keep these people, the job must remain as interesting, challenging, and fun as it was originally sold. Marketing people talk constantly about creating a "compelling value proposition" for their customers. Can you give your current and future employees the same promise that you'd give your customers—namely, a reason to buy? The people you want on your team want to join a compelling vision, work for a compelling leader, work with compelling people, and do compelling work. From your perch, can you do what it takes to make this the case, and thus compete for the best talent in your space?

As followers we are willing to be enrolled. We are waiting to be led. We are compelled by our leaders and by the opportunities that they see and pursue. But we must believe that this place we wish to join is a place where our best work can emerge. Finally, if we are going to sacrifice our time, treasure, and the chance for something even better, we need to know that our leaders value and trust us as much as we are expected to value and trust them.

And if we are expected to accomplish something great, then we expect our leaders to commit to greatness. All the way.

Are you ready, as a leader, to make that commitment?

The Essentials of Being Compelling

- No one is obligated to follow you; it is an "opt-in" world for the best and brightest—the rainmakers and value drivers in your organization.
- To feel compelled requires identifying with a cause. Recruit A Players through a big vision of the future and a personal commitment to a mission in which those who join can see a place for their contribution.
- You must earn and keep the attention and commitment of your best people. You are competing for mindshare. You need them more than they need you.
- People want honest communication and a meaningful challenge, not an easy job. Remember the power of self-interest: What's in it for me?
- Stand on your own commitment to inspire and evoke emotion in others. You will be seen as compelling. There is nothing that inspires like a leader's complete commitment to the vision—and to winning.

PART TWO

COMPETENCE
Leading on the Field with Skill

Welcome to game day. As anyone who has ever competed in organized sports knows, there is a very big difference between all of those hours at practice, in the weight room, and studying game films—and that moment, as the crowd cheers, when you step between the lines on opening day or walk up to the first tee and play for a score. Now it's *real*. The score counts. And you either win or lose.

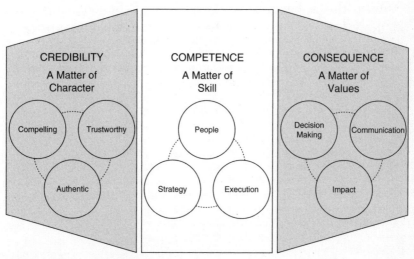

Figure P2.1. A Matter of Skill

Leadership is a game too, but one that can have immense, even fatal, consequences. And great leaders are the people who know how to play and win. They not only have in place all of the prerequisites of Unusually Excellent leadership I described in Part One, but they also have the courage, the presence of mind, and the competence to model them in real time, in the midst of the confusion and fog of battle and facing very real consequences for their decisions.

If the preparation for leadership is the development of character, its execution is a matter of *skills*: the skills to lead people through the challenges of both failure and success, the skills to create and execute a strategy that recognizes both the team's strengths and limitations, and the skills to execute operations in order to achieve those strategic goals. In many ways, leading people, strategy, and execution is improvisational symphony—the coordination of multiple groups of professionals, playing the same music, in harmony, but with the added twist that something could unexpectedly interrupt the performance—and you'll have to improvise on the fly and still make it sound perfect. To carry this metaphor further, your job is not to play any of the instruments, or even to write the music; it is to lead the group to its best performance—and you are the one who is paid to know what it is supposed to sound like.

With this as background, I suggest that the most important question that every leader in the midst of leading must answer is this:

What are the required leadership skills you will need to successfully get the job done?

● CHAPTER FOUR

LEADING PEOPLE
Talent to Teams

> Hire people who are better than you are, then leave
> them to get on with it. Look for people who will
> aim for the remarkable, who will not settle for
> the routine.
>
> —*David Ogilvy*

very business is a "people" business, because every business—
indeed, every meaningful endeavor—is composed of human
beings taking action in an organized manner to accomplish the mission in front of them. To get this chapter started properly, I'll restate
something that you have probably heard before but that I believe is
even more true today than it has ever been—*there is no substitute
for talent*. To be even more accurate—there is no substitute for the
best talent you can find and hire. It may seem obvious, but let's
review this idea. Why do we want the best talent?

For starters, we know that most organizations are limited by—
or propelled to success primarily by—the quality of the people on
the team. From an NFL football franchise, to a business of any size,
shape or flavor, to a nonprofit or community organization, the best
teams separate themselves from the pack primarily by having more
capable, talented, committed people.

The corollary to this idea is that the better the talent, the better the results. There are some notable exceptions to this principle—like the 1988 U.S. Olympic hockey team—a group of very average hockey players who won the gold medal. But in the vast majority of situations, the more talented the team at every position, the more likely it is to meet its strategic goals. Hiring great people is arguably the highest-leverage activity that leaders undertake, and it is common to find highly respected, successful leaders spending up to half their time engaged in issues around talent, team, expectations, and performance coaching. They know the payoff can be substantial for the investment they make in people. There have been thousands of challenges to this principle—made in the hope that it wasn't so true that talent matters so much. Most, if not all of these experiments have failed, leading us back to the opening assertion: the quality of the people around you sets the tone and determines the probability of success in almost any endeavor undertaken.

High performers set a different standard; they raise the bar for everyone. If you want to raise the performance of your team, start by hiring one person who performs at a level different from that of your current group. You will soon see the performance of the whole team move up. Then find another person of that caliber and hire her. The best people in any profession want to work with peers of the same caliber.

Seating Chart

You'll know the truth about a job—how it is really supposed to be done and the possibility it represents within the organization—only when the right person is doing it. Most of the time, we complain about something not getting done and don't realize—or don't want to see—that the real problem is we have the wrong person in that job. Nothing changes the results in a functional role faster, or more dramatically, than getting the right person doing the work. A job turns from a liability to an asset as soon as the right person takes over. As the great business writer Jim Collins reminds us in *Good to Great*, we have to "get the right people in the right seats on the bus."

What distinguishes the kind of talent that can move the needle in a different way than most other people can? Talent follows the normal Pareto 80/20 principle—20 percent of your team produces 80 percent of the organization's value and ability to execute competitively. The shorthand for this group of people is "value creators" or the "best and brightest." In some companies, they are identified as HIPOs—high performance/high potential. They are the people that you'd want to recruit from your own team if you left to start a competitive venture. And, if you were honest about it, you'd say that out of every hundred people, there are between fifteen and twenty-five who would be obvious and automatic priority choices if you were to cherry-pick your own team. These are *rainmakers*—people in every functional area who, against the odds, just always make things happen. You need these people—and you know what they look like because you have some of them now. Any time you have the chance to get a few more, you should do anything you can to make it happen. Don't wait for an opening to bring this kind of talent on board. Find the people, and make a spot for them. You'll never regret hiring the best people you can find.

We have reviewed the basics of why talent matters so much to the performance and success of organizations. What is the rest of the leader's agenda regarding *people*?

- Hire the best
- Focus on "fit"
- Make it a team
- Lead that team to victory

As I noted earlier, Unusually Excellent leaders take hiring seriously and personally. They are involved in the *design* of the hiring process, including the interviewing process (which most people have never been trained to do properly), and, they pride themselves on personally meeting every candidate headed for an offer, if it is humanly possible to do so. They are on the hunt, constantly and relentlessly, for talented people—using every resource available to (1) identify the people they should know and (2) get to know them. They are always networking and always selling their company— meeting people who could lead them to the superstars, whether they are active in the market or not.

Great leaders earn that title by having the self-assurance to *always* do their very best to hire people who are smarter than they are—for real. They are secure in their role and their leadership equity and are genuinely not threatened by talent—on the contrary, they crave having world-class people, knowing that the bar goes up each time a super-talented person joins the team. They really want that team of all-stars—one in every slot on the team— and they will work diligently toward that goal. Some leaders must think a sub-par team makes them look better, because those are the kinds of people they hire and keep in place, often in spite of coaching from the outside to upgrade the team. In my experience in venture capital, more time at board meetings was spent discussing the caliber of the team than on any other topic. Unusually Excellent leaders know that a world-class team makes them look better—and more important, helps them succeed.

But recruiting and keeping that kind of talent takes considerable effort, self-assurance, even bravery. If you hire the best people to follow you, they are going to demand the best from the people around them. And if you aren't up to the job of leading them, they will let you know, by telling you in both obvious and subtle ways— and if you don't listen, they'll leave.

The most talented job applicants in the world are a bad choice if they are not going to fit with you, your team, and the culture that you've built—indeed, if they don't fit, they are actually a handicap. There is no one so talented that you'd risk the team chemistry to hire a misfit or a disruptive prima donna. By the same token, a top applicant's considerable talents are useless to you if the person is not a good match with that role and responsibility and, to a lesser degree, a specific place in the structure of the organization. Each of us has a "sweet spot" for our talent, a "power alley" where we can make our greatest contribution to an operation. Most people live to do good work and love to do good work, and we want to set them up to win, but we should be careful to avoid setting the expectation that we are running a career training center. Hire people into something at which they can excel; later, if warranted, you can expand their territory. Find talent that fits, then grow it to greatness.

As you proceed, remember: People are imperfect, even those talented people you do hire. They are human, and they will occasionally have issues that you may know about—and some you may not. Leaders are in the people business; they will eventually find themselves face-to-face with people problems and people's problems—and the two *are* different. I advise you to embrace those opportunities, without overmanaging them, and make sure your team members, to a person, know they can be honest and forthright with you, especially when they hit a pothole in their life. Most of these kinds of issues get better when attended to and worse when ignored. These are the kinds of issues that age more like bananas than like fine wine—they don't get better with time.

If the prospect of this responsibility to engage with what comes with the territory—people—doesn't appeal to you; if you aren't willing to interact with people on a personal basis when required, then don't be a doctor, a psychologist, a marriage counselor—or a leader. Those jobs are fundamentally about people and everything that makes people who they are. You can't have the good without a bit of the bad or the ugly, which may emerge unpredictably at inconvenient and sometimes unfortunate times. Bring compassion, patience, empathy, and understanding to these moments—along with a clear sense of where your role in a business or an organization stops when it comes to these kinds of challenges.

Finally, one of the sticky questions about people: which matters more, talent or team? The answer is *both*. History reminds us over and over that although some notable individuals often get the public recognition, most achievements of significance were accomplished by a team—be it landing on the moon, scaling Everest, or winning the Super Bowl. There is always a team behind great results, even if they aren't in the limelight. Even the greatest visionaries need support, if only in the dissemination and application of their ideas. Although talent is key, teams that work together are the heart and soul of high-performance organizations.

People First

Jim Collins has some strong opinions about hiring. His message is the *Who First* principle: "First who, then what."

What he means is that your first priority should be hiring the very best people; only then should you focus on building the right plan for the organization. In one respect, this seems a reasonable strategy—after all, if you don't have the talent, the chances of executing successfully are slim. But on the other, if you don't have a plan, how are you going to convince people to join you? And how do you know if you are hiring the right people for the job if you don't know what the job is?

For those obvious reasons, most leaders resist the Who First principle because they don't feel like they can go find great people until they have a strategy to pitch. But they are wrong. Why? Because the best people aren't primarily attracted to a strategy; they are intrigued more by a compelling vision and mission. Moreover, those great people you don't have yet? You need them in order to build a great strategy. Finally, the best people will construct not only the best strategy for the firm, but one that has a place for them in it—and there is nothing better than a great plan, build by super-talented people, who have designed themselves into the accountability for results.

So when you are recruiting, don't recruit to your strategy. Recruit to mission and vision, then let *them—the great people you've hired*—help you develop the right strategy. That's what they want to do. Let them.

Let me tell you a story to illustrate this philosophy.

Get the Talent, Then Make the Plan

I know a CEO who, although happily semi-retired, was convinced by an old friend who was a board member of a troubled company to lace up his cleats and get back on the field to do the one thing he had never done before—a turnaround. Not surprisingly, he arrived to find not only a broken business but also a classic "B team" executive staff. Worse, he inherited this team after the company had been in a long period of decline and had filed for protection under the Chapter 11 bankruptcy laws. The challenge was clear for the new CEO—get this company through the legalities of the bankruptcy process, then restore it back to the prominence it once enjoyed. The customers were incredibly loyal, the products were in demand, and the technology was still relevant. The mistakes of the past stemmed mostly from hubris and mismanagement, and that would not happen again.

As a tactical necessity, the CEO worked with the board of directors to put in place a nine-month incentive plan to keep this team in place during the course of the bankruptcy—the idea was to create stability with the employee base and consistency with customers as the new, revived company was being designed and built. In other words, the message to the execs was: *Don't leave. You may not be a high performer, but you have the knowledge of the past and I need that for the future. I need stability.*

The incentive worked, and while the CEO spent an incredible amount of time with lawyers and accountants for the ensuing nine months to get the company's financials restructured, the execs kept the business "stable"—but did not move the company towards a new level of capability whatsoever. When the CEO returned to full-time operations, it was obvious that it was time to go find and hire the A team, because he knew, intellectually, a universal truth: *nothing changes in the game until we change the players.* But, surprisingly, the CEO struggled to make the necessary changes. In so many words, he told me: *I'm not ready yet. I've been away dealing with the bankruptcy stuff, so it's like I'm still brand-new here. I don't have a plan yet, much less a strategy. I can't start hiring until I know what I'm doing.*

Unfortunately, this CEO didn't seem to fully appreciate the hole he was digging for himself. With only fatigued and disillusioned executives surrounding him—many of whom had been on the team that had sunk the previous ship—he was hamstrung to create real change. The only way he could create a top-notch revival plan for the company would be if he *wrote the whole thing himself*. This CEO was both blessed and cursed by his substantial experience in what we'll call "tactical" recruiting—in other words, selling The Plan to candidates and finding people to join a well-established strategy. But tactical recruiting in a company without a great plan is the proverbial shuffling of the deck chairs on the Titanic. The CEO needed to recruit the best warriors into his new crusade and let them build the recovery plan. Unfortunately, this CEO is not a born crusader; he is a battlefield commander. So by insisting on designing his plan first, he had put himself into a vicious cycle. Without a plan, he couldn't hire the team. Without a team, he wouldn't get a plan. Ouch.

What should this CEO have done? As uncomfortable as it might have felt, he needed to make recruiting and building a top-shelf team his first priority. Go recruit people purely with the vision and the message that this is going to be the greatest turnaround in the history of Silicon Valley. Find people who are compelled by something different—something unusual—a once-in-a-lifetime opportunity to save something that can be great again. Tell them that the financial community has knocked this stock down so far that there's nowhere to go but up—and into their pockets. Tell them, "Hey, we have some great technology here—and now we're going to reinvent this thing and rise up out of the ashes." Explain that they can be part of the team that will be forever known as having saved a legendary company from ultimate demise and led that company back to prominence. That this is something you can tell your kids. *That's* recruiting to a cause, to a mission, to a vision—and not waiting for a strategy. And once these talented folks were settled into place, the CEO could say: "Now, ladies and gentlemen, let's build a great plan and strategy for realizing our bold vision."

The E's of People Leadership

So we've made the case for paying permanent attention to hiring world-class talent wherever and whenever you can find it. And for paying attention to fit, structure, and culture to ensure early productivity. Day to day, leaders lead people to achieve the purpose of their organization, and leading people has its own *five E's* of skills—though by comparison to those associated with *being compelling*, these are much more action-oriented. Let's look at the essentials of leading the great people you've found and hired.

Engagement

Once you've assembled your team, your biggest test as a leader is to motivate each member of that team to become fully committed to the success of your project. You've chosen them for their talents, and for the alignment of those talents to the task at hand. You've also placed them into positions where those talents can have the greatest impact. The challenge now is to spark each of those individuals into action, so that they contribute at the highest possible level.

That can happen only if each of these team members is fully engaged in the project. And that, in turn, can occur only if you are engaged with them in their success.

How do you do that? Well, you've already begun by making your full public commitment to the project. This not only sets a high standard (and level of expectation) for the other team members, but just as important, it makes it safe for them to fully commit as well. As you've no doubt already experienced from your own career, *nobody* wants to be played for a sucker—and that begins with committing yourself more to a project than to the boss.

But as leader your engagement goes still further. Your job is to be not only fully engaged in your own success and that of the project but also in the work and career of each individual member of that project. You do that by personally connecting with each team member on a regular basis. In the case of a larger organization, you perform this regular engagement with your lieutenants—and then require them to do the same with their subordinates all the way down the organization.

You also engage people by setting realistic goals with them and fairly rewarding them for meeting or exceeding those expectations. Many leaders treat this part of the job casually—and that can be a dangerous mistake. The team member who feels that he or she is being forced to meet an impossible goal, or who believes he or she has not been sufficiently recognized for achieving a goal, feels betrayed and can quickly become resentful, unproductive, and a management problem. It almost goes without saying that it is often your most talented employees who are the quickest to react this way.

Enrollment

Every team project, big or small, is a crusade. It has a goal, a strategy for getting to that goal, and a series of tactics to execute that strategy. And there is one more variable: the people who must join that crusade.

Whatever the ultimate rewards at the successful completion of that crusade, at the beginning of the journey there are only costs and sacrifices. At a minimum, these costs include time and opportunity. If you are part of a start-up enterprise, it may also mean lost income to leave a more stable, high compensation job elsewhere.

It is during these early days that enrollment is hardest to achieve. The transition to the new program is difficult and the shakedown of operations distracting. The cost/benefit ratio is typically at its worst, and eventual success is both far off and of unknown likelihood. And no one on the team has yet accumulated enough time and experience on the project to feel the kind of commitment that will come later. However, this is the time when a compelling leader, with a mission that matters, can rise above these challenges and get a team fully invested in the mission. Organizations and groups throughout history have tried to overcome these early-day obstacles and slow starts to the learning curve by creating rituals and communal activities to tie new members to the group as closely and as quickly as possible. In the most extreme cases—as with cults, fraternities, and secret societies—these rituals can include initiation rites and even physical transformation (such as tattoos and clothing colors). Join the military, and you will lose your hair, gain a uniform, and be required to take an oath with enormous legal implications. Become a citizen, and you will be required to take a public oath of allegiance.

But even for the most informal group, such as a product group or sales team or school faculty, there remain basic processes that *enroll* you into that group. It can range from a name badge and new email address to a regular Friday afternoon beer bust to the act of signing a formal statement of nondisclosure of the group's intellectual property. The obvious reason for all of this is team-building, combined with a certain amount of security. But another, hidden purpose is to make it more difficult for the new team member to leave—buying time until other gravitational forces come into play.

Expectations

Hiring world-class talent drives higher standards; the job of leadership is to make sure those standards are met. The process of establishing standards should begin, as we've already noted, during the hiring process. You have hired your team based on three basic criteria: the fit between their talents and your needs, the values they share with the rest of the team, and your belief that over time they will align well with the culture of your team.

These criteria instantly create their own attendant expectations—that is, that the new team member will meet them, and quickly. But there are other expectations that will also, over time, be placed on this team member—most of them dealing with either performance milestones or career development. A third, usually implicit, expectation over time will deal with the behavior of the team member: that it be both in accordance with the team's official rules and congruent with the team's culture.

As a leader, it is absolutely crucial that you remove as many gray areas—that is, areas of future dispute—from this process as possible. Obviously, you cannot remove them all—we're dealing with the messiness of human nature here, after all—but you can spare yourself and your team a lot of future grief by making your expectations very clear and understood.

If there is a minimum level of performance below which a team member cannot drop and still remain with the group, tell them up front—rather than look arbitrary or even vindictive by announcing your rule at the moment you enforce it. If your rules of behavior and the consequences of violating them are precise, codified, and distributed to every team member, then if they are violated you have not only the strongest possible case but also the support of the other team members.

Energy

We spoke of enthusiasm as a key leader characteristic in the *being compelling* step. Enthusiasm converts to action over the course of project. We tend to conflate "energy" with "energetic"—and, of course, that is one of the characteristics of a great leader. But energy takes a lot of different forms when it comes to leadership.

One form might be called *relationship energy*. We've all known this type of leader: the hearty handshake, the loud voice, the ability to remember hundreds of names and faces seemingly forever, the talent for making people want to join whatever cause or campaign is being offered. All of us have experienced leaders with so much relational energy that they are off-putting—but you may also note that those same people are often quite successful. There are times that someone else's energy can inspire our own, and suddenly we are more alive and ready to go than we were just a moment ago.

A second form can be called *functional energy*. These are leaders who always seem crisp, engaged, and focused, even when they are physically exhausted or mentally weary. When others fade, these leaders seem to find hidden reservoirs of energy. Jack Welch of General Electric was famous for having this sort of Ironman energy.

I believe the most valuable form is *emotional energy*. When the going gets toughest, and success seems most elusive, lesser souls either despair or look for an exit strategy. But great leaders find their deep pools of emotional energy to spur themselves on and remain focused, engaged, and optimistic. History's most admired leaders—from warriors like Lee, to statesmen like Lincoln, to social activists like King—have shown almost supernatural emotional energy.

Finally, there is *career energy*. The importance of this type of energy usually becomes obvious only on the back nine of a long career. Young leaders, precisely because they are young, tend to be profligate with their own energy. They assume that they will always be able to work themselves nearly to death—and then quickly recover to start again. But older leaders either learn to shepherd their strength and save it for the moments when it is most needed, or they burn out and depart.

It takes a long time to get to the top. The typical U.S. president, four-star general, Fortune 50 CEO, or foundation chairman achieves that position after thirty or forty years of hard work, and at an age when most of their weary contemporaries are dreaming of retirement. We'll look at this further in Part Three, but for the purpose of this chapter, the point is that leadership energy is not just for expending now, but must be paced in expectation of a long career.

Empowerment

You have located and engaged the best talent, established your vision of success, enrolled your team as energetic participants in the crusade, and set standards and expectations for their success. You have also brought yourself, heart and soul, to the project.

You have done all of that well, even brilliantly. But you will still fail if you do not take the final step: you need to delegate your power and distribute your authority to empower others to get the job done.

Shelves of books have been written in the last two decades about this paradox—that the more power you give up, the more power you seem to retain. That this is so, we'll just assume for now. I want to address the *process* of empowerment.

Empowerment is essentially the exercise of authority and power by divesting oneself of much of that authority and power. This is not done in a vacuum. We have discussed in detail the cultural environment and character of the leader that makes distributed leadership really work.

It began with authenticity and trustworthiness: that is, you've shown that you have the power and authority, you deserve to have them, and you can be trusted to transfer both of them without risk of your arbitrarily taking them back.

Next, you've recruited members of your team based on their ability—that is, you've already established that they can handle this new power. Further, you've set standards for behavior and performance in which these newly designated leaders can exercise their authority without the danger of their going rogue.

Finally, you've established channels of communication and relationships of trust and respect with your subordinates so that you each understand the others goals, motives and interests, so that you can combine for the maximum effectiveness.

What is needed now, in the final step of the empowerment process, is the establishment of feedback loops and performance coaching. The feedback recognizes that you are ultimately responsible for everything that takes place below you in the organization—therefore you need to be able to monitor the performance of others, identify early warnings, and make sure the entire team remains in balance.

Performance coaching recognizes that no leader is supremely competent in every aspect of his or her profession—so leaders need to look elsewhere for advice, training, best practices, and acquired wisdom. This is particularly true for young and new leaders—who, no matter what their natural skills, may not be able to meet your performance expectations without some outside support.

Retreat to Attack

There is an organization I know well, based in New York, called Endeavor, that does amazing work enabling and supporting entrepreneurs in developing economies around the globe. I have done some advisory work with the global Endeavor team, and it is, to say the least, an impressive organization, with a big vision.

Endeavor's mission is to establish and operate entrepreneurial support systems in developing countries—such as Chile, Brazil, Columbia, Argentina, Turkey, Greece, and Egypt—where there are a lot of great entrepreneurs but an inadequate financial and professional infrastructure to help them build robust companies. Endeavor's goal is to assist "high impact" entrepreneurs—those with the potential of changing the national GDP by 1 percent.

With time and experience, Endeavor has realized that the absolute key factor in the success of these in-country support systems is the creation of an in-country board of advisors that includes the most influential business executives and government leaders in that country. The highly successful business people in each country—many of whom have built great companies, industrial conglomerates, or holding companies, and who are now in a position in their lives where their success is assured—now see as their legacy helping the next generation of young business people. All that Endeavor asks of these board members is that they be *available and supportive—to offer their wisdom and share their contacts and relationships*. They lend their credibility to an entrepreneur by telling others: *Hey, I've met these guys, I've seen their plan, and in my professional opinion they deserve the chance to make it.*

The flip side of this is that the actual support that Endeavor has chosen to give is not money (that's been tried and failed in the past), but *access* to capital sources and strategic advisory support at the highest levels in the country. Thus, to be selected by Endeavor—a fairly arduous and rigorous selection process that takes anywhere from three months to two years—is like getting the Good Housekeeping Seal of Approval as an entrepreneur. Once blessed by Endeavor, many doors open that were previously closed.

In other words, Endeavor has built a brand image around its value-add—and that brand says "We vetted the entrepreneurs in this country, and these are the best ones." Its core business strategy is to study a potential country carefully, identify both the likely entrepreneurs and the candidates for the board, then build the board simultaneously with the entrepreneur selection process. A key element of this strategy is to sell the cause and the mission—not the plan. The people Endeavor wants on these local boards don't need a structured plan—these local business veterans want to help build the Endeavor presence in their country with their own flair and spin. All they need is a *cause* to which they can hitch their emotional commitment to make a difference, a cause they can include in their own legacy. The Endeavor mission is just such a cause, and thus can attract amazing people to the opportunity.

Over five years ago, the Endeavor team decided to target Turkey as its next high-potential country for assisted entrepreneurship. Unfortunately, it was not the best time for that country—a change in government, ethnic strife, and a financial crisis were all contributing to the country's instability. However, that seemed all the more reason to enter the country and build a local organization and presence.

But the Endeavor team soon realized that at that point, no matter how hard they tried, they just couldn't attract the right people for the Turkish board. Now they had a choice: stay the course and help the worthy Turkish entrepreneurs they had already begun to identify, or abort the mission. With great humility, and some humiliation, they bravely chose the latter—knowing from experience that without the right board, they were likely doomed to failure. The decision to pull out came with some public embarrassment to Endeavor. It was a courageous, principled decision.

Endeavor returned to Turkey three years later. The situation there had improved tremendously. Meanwhile, Endeavor had acquired even more credibility, more scale, and more contacts, including the names of more good Turkish entrepreneurs. Most important, they now had credible introductions and references to a group of the most influential business people and families in Turkey. My, how much had changed in three short years. The time was now right—but mostly because they could attract the best people in the country to join their team as a local board, which created countless advantages for the entrepreneurs that would be chosen in the normal, high-quality selection process that Endeavor had perfected in other parts of the globe. Endeavor Turkey now has one of the very best in-country boards and, as a direct result, some of the finest entrepreneurs in the world, growing and thriving, due in no small part to the support they get from these local icons.

The lesson for the entire Endeavor organization, and one that has served them elsewhere since, was that as frustrating and disappointing as it was to not be able to charge in and meet a perceived need in a market, it was far better to wait until they could attract the very best people and get them in place to execute that strategy. With the right people in place, it all worked, whereas it would have failed before. It is better to leave the kitchen than to ruin the meal.

Final Questions

I'll close this chapter, the first of three steps in this part about leadership competence in action, with a series of people questions that you should ask yourself—and regularly ask again—throughout the course of your career as a leader.

How Has the Nature of Your Enterprise Changed?

You've built your team based on their best fit with the challenge at hand. But what if that challenge has changed? Do your team members still fit—or should they be moved, retrained, or replaced?

A classic example of this challenge is the new entrepreneurial start-up that proves wildly successful and decides to become a public company. Those employees who devoted almost everything to the founding and creation of this enterprise—the creative and adaptive founders—often find there is no place for them in the new more conservative and bureaucratic public company. This is often the most traumatic time in a company's history, despite the sizable financial reward to those same founders.

But it cannot be helped. Success, just as much as failure, brings change. As a leader, if you have not prepared your people for that change or you resist that change, you have failed in your responsibilities.

Where Is Your Authority or Positional Power Best Used in Leading People?

Your leadership clout is best applied to setting expectations with all the key members of your team, and to creating the process to build real teamwork. This allows a standard of behavior and performance among your best and brightest people to set the bar higher for everyone. This is the area where you can truly garner a nonlinear result from your investment of time and emotional energy. By carefully and thoughtfully setting performance expectations with your key team members that, collectively, create a higher standard of expected results, you have moved the whole game up a notch or two. This work on your part pays dividends for years to come; it is the groundwork you have to lay to build a truly high-performance culture. It all starts in the conversation with your team about what you expect, and what they can reasonably (or unreasonably) deliver.

What Is Your Plan to Deal with Your Weakest Link?

Even on a team of all-stars, someone is going to be the worst performer. The other half of Jim Collins' "get the right people in the right seats on the bus" talk is not as well known—he says, "Get the wrong people off the bus." Do you have a strategy for dealing with chronic underperformers? Some organizations have a policy, written or unwritten, of regularly removing performers in the lowest 10 percent. Others deal with it on a case-by-case basis—after all, if your team really is a group of superstars, that worst performer might still be better than any replacement out there in the world. There is nothing else in business that will cause you headaches like the ones you will suffer from failing to move a problem child off the playground. This is a case in which ignorance is definitely not bliss, and denial leads to more pain, for everyone, as times goes on.

How you deal with these weakest links is ultimately less important than having a fundamental awareness of the issue and a plan for taking action. And making your criteria known to everyone on the team—and *sticking to it*. Failing to warn, censure, punish, or fire a poorly performing subordinate because you haven't the guts to do it is a failure of *you* as a leader—and worthy of the same fate you should be imposing on them. The worst part is that everyone knows who the weak team members are, and at some point the joke is on you, Mr. or Ms. Leader, for acting far too late. Ideally you'll see these situations emerge before they become common knowledge and, from there, chronic problems. That's not to say you can't be a great leader if you can't punish and fire your followers. Here in Silicon Valley, some of the most famous executives in our history haven't had the stomach for that task. What they did instead was find that subordinate who did have the personality for the job. Of course, in doing so they sacrificed some of their authority to that "hatchet man"—but it worked. I don't recommend that strategy—not only is it the chicken way out, but it also undermines your own vital authenticity. I merely note that it can sometimes be made to work as an exception to standard policy, especially in a special situation where the chemistry between a leader and the person who needs to move on is just not healthy enough to tolerate the needed action.

The worst scenario of all is to have a plan for dealing with underperformers, execute it to identify who those individuals are, and then *not* pull the trigger on the announced consequences, for reasons of sentimentality, weakness, or favoritism—or, worst of all, an attempt to preserve leadership popularity. *Nothing* can be more damaging to the morale and esprit de corps of a team than that kind of leadership. It destroys your authenticity, your trustworthiness, and your ability to compel others to act. It is the end of you as a leader. Indeed, it is better to have no weakest-link plan at all than one with obvious liabilities.

How Will You Distinguish the Bad Performer from a Bad Plan?

Almost as bad as refusing to punish underperformance is punishing good employees who have failed because they were required to execute a bad plan. We've already discussed the vital role that a sense of safety plays among followers: it frees them to devote all of their energies to the task, it liberates them to be innovative, and it produces a healthy sense of teamwork.

Strip away that trust—and there is no faster way than to blame a team member who did his or her best on a bad project—and just the opposite occurs: paranoid employees hunkered down, trying not to do anything that might attract attention.

As a leader, you have to think like a venture capitalist, with your project leaders as the entrepreneurs and the project itself a new venture. If that venture fails, you are deficient as a leader if you do not look past the mere fact of success and failure to ask the all-important question: *Why did the project fail?* This postmortem must always occur, because only then will you gain the knowledge you need both to determine blame and to learn for the next project.

Needless to say, part of this process is to get your own ego out of the way. On the one hand, if the failed project was your idea, it can be very difficult not to blame the project leader—after all, how can the failure be the fault of your brilliant idea? But in fact, as often as not, the project itself really was to blame. And you can console yourself with the knowledge that admitting your own error will only enhance your image with your followers.

On the other hand, if the project leader did in fact fail, you need to continue your inquiry to ask whether the leader failed because of his or her own poor performance or because the leader chose the wrong team for the job. Either way, it may be a good leadership decision to keep that person and train him or her to be better at one or the other of those tasks.

What Is Your Power Alley?

I'll close the chapter with this one final question. We've devoted a lot of pages to looking at the nature of followers, how you choose teams, and how you find the best fit between your subordinates and the task before you. But let us not forget that, as leader, you too are a member of the team and subject to all of the rules and standards of the group. If you are going to narrow your selection process to those desirable potential team members whose strongest skills and aptitudes—their power alleys—are precisely congruent with the needs of the team, then you also need to turn that microscope on yourself. Are you the best person to lead this team, on this project, toward this goal?

You had best ask yourself this question at the beginning of the campaign—and regularly thereafter. And if at any point your answer is "no," then you owe it to yourself and to the people around you to either refuse the job or, if it is already under way, find your replacement.

Leading people is often what we really mean when we use the word *leadership*, and it may suffice to leave the definition of leadership specific and narrow and let everything else in this book serve as a derivative of the people part of the job. No other chapter could serve as a replacement for the title of the book, except this one.

The Essentials of Leading People

- Commit to hiring the best people you can possibly find. This is one thing about which you should be maniacal. *Talent* and *team* are different, and both are crucial. Fit is key—that is, the fit with the organization's values and culture and, sometimes, structure. Don't allow fit to mean "people just like me."

- Don't wait until you have a perfect plan to seek the best people. The best people aren't compelled by a plan—they want to help build it. These kinds of people are attracted to a *cause* and they want to join *you.*

- Find people who are, by their nature, aligned with the cultural values and the spirit of the mission. You should not believe you will be able to substantially change people from who they are, fundamentally. (*Some say that men marry women hoping they won't change and women marry men hoping they can change them—and both are disappointed.*)

- Get people in their power alley—that is the only way you'll know about the real job to be done and the real capabilities of the person.

- Choosing, motivating, and setting expectations with key people is the highest leverage work that leaders do— everything else in the organization follows from there. The difference between a superstar and a misfit can be the delta between a dream and a nightmare.

CHAPTER FIVE

LEADING STRATEGY
Ideas to Plans

What's the use in running if you are on the
wrong road?

—*German proverb*

All men can see these tactics whereby I conquer,
but what none can see is the strategy out of which
victory is evolved.

—*Sun Tzu*

Strategy is a word that we hear used often—mostly in a casual and imprecise manner, as shorthand for explaining that we have a thoughtful, measured attack plan to solve day-to-day problems. We have *strategies* for everything—from finding the best price on orange juice or airline tickets to getting home at a reasonable hour in the rush hour commute. And our use of this concept, as a part of the modern social discourse, is generally correct—for our proposed method to get something done—something we care about that requires some thinking or planning beyond our normal working knowledge, natural instincts, reactive intuition, or applied life experience.

In the real world, under the pressure of command, leaders regularly confuse or collapse the distinctions among leading people, strategy, and execution. They sometimes assume that because they have the right people and a distinct goal that they can simply "flood the zone" and find success. Or they believe that a single-minded focus on day-to-day tactics, yet another "two yards and a cloud of dust," will eventually deliver them to their destination. But *strategy* is one essential leg of the three-legged stool that is *competence* (as evidenced by its chapter position in this part of the book: leading people, leading *strategy*, and leading execution), and it is equally as important as the other two disciplines. A successful performance is not just the musicians, nor the playing of the music; it is also the sheet music on the stand—the *plan* for the notes and chords that allows talented people to make it sound so good.

It is often said that everything is created twice—once in the mind and once in the world. So to make a dream or a vision come true, we must first imagine it, but then we must make a plan—only then can we build it. And to create something serious, we likely need a serious strategy. Smart people don't initiate complex or large-scale projects, where there is money at stake, without a real plan. Strategy becomes even more crucial when organizations become substantial in revenue or people, or the business competes in multiple product lines and geographies, or the nature of the mission is inherently complex. Paradoxically, organizations like this often need a much simpler plan than they imagine.

Even those leaders who recognize the distinction and understand the vital role of a good strategy in creating results sometimes suffer from *hammer-nail syndrome*. That is, if all they have is a hammer, everything looks like a nail. In my experience, many leaders often see the people challenges with a clear view, even if the fixes are occasionally unpleasant and great talent is tough to find. Most leaders are also clear about the importance of execution, as that's been their power alley the whole of their career. So people often view strategy as amorphous and mysterious, difficult to create and communicate and implement. Done by "strategists," which they aren't. They let their natural talents in team building and action taking dominate their leadership mind-set. Strategy gets short shrift. Sometimes they assume that because they have a *business plan*, it inevitably follows that they have a business strategy. Some conflate a marketing strategy or a sales strategy or a manufacturing strategy—believing that the proper execution of one will serve as the strategy for all. In reality, if these different strategies aren't aligned to each other, they can actually produce dismal results and pull the organization apart.

Process to Plans

Unusually Excellent leaders appreciate the power of a plan. They realize that even the best athletes need a playbook, a game plan, or a pre-shot routine to ensure that their talent shows up on the field. Surgeons, pilots, lawyers, practitioners of any profession where the work is complex always have a plan—even if the task is something they've done hundreds of times before. They also know that great plans are created from accurate and complete data gathering, a rigorous analytical process, and the collaborative efforts of experienced and wise people. And the most important thing they know is that although the *content* of brilliant plans is the domain of sophisticated data and creative thinking, the art of *leading strategy* is a *process competency*—a skill that great leaders continuously sharpen. They realize that great plans develop from vigorous conversations, among the best people they can gather, and then are endorsed and driven from the top. They know that a good plan must capture the best ideas of the organization in innovative and bold ways, mostly from the bottom up. Most of all, they understand that without a plan to win, they are left with only a plan to lose.

That said, a plan—no matter how brilliant—is not a strategy. A strategy is bigger than a plan. After all is said and done, a plan is an intellectual construction that combines the best information that can be gathered about what is so now, thoughtful predictions about what will happen in the future, and a model for how to succeed in light of those conditions. A strategy includes this plan but also accounts for *how* we do things, not just *what* we'll do—and it accounts for what happens when that plan collides with reality.

A strategy is the next, penultimate step in the process that begins with a vision, that then becomes a formal plan, and only then, in light of changing events, plays out as a strategy. As we'll see in Chapter Six, Leading Execution, that strategy, when put into practice, produces measurable results—with *tactics* as the short-term response to unexpected contingencies. A great plan, as it evolves into a great strategy, also presents the opportunity for the crucial performance variables to be measured and discussed—the core requirement for managing execution.

Unusually Excellent leaders thrive on knowing their game plan at all times. They are fluent in the basics of that plan—and they recognize the value of a good plan. They also know how much their teams count on them to articulate that plan, again and again. And in many cases there are operating principles or brand statements within the organization that frame and reinforce those plan basics.

A TaylorMade Philosophy

TaylorMade-adidas Golf (TMaG) has grown to well over a billion dollars in sales at a 15-percent annual rate of growth over the last seven years—at a time when the rest of the industry has been growing 5 percent or less per year. TMaG is without a doubt one of the most successful and dominant companies in the sports equipment world. It doesn't take a genius to figure out that they have taken massive amounts of market share from their competitors over this time frame to enjoy that growth rate.

One reason the company has been so successful is that CEO Mark King and his team created what amounts to a brand statement that also serves as its day-to-day corporate strategy. A paraphrase: *To be the best performance golf brand in the world, we must design and build products for proficient and aspirational golfers, and validate that promise through broad adoption by the best professional players in the world.* Period.

In other words, the TaylorMade strategy needed to be to know everything about and then build the world's best products for people who believe that golf is a *sport*, not a game. People who believe that equipment *matters*. And people who see themselves as *athletes*, not recreational players. If you don't see how profoundly different these two camps are, then you are not a serious golfer.

From this simple yet powerful statement of purpose, almost everything TMaG does directly follows. Against this distinct profile of proficient and aspirational players who demand the best, Taylor-Made tests every product idea, every marketing strategy, and every sales strategy.

Then TaylorMade turns around and validates this strategy by engaging the largest group of the best players in the world to use their products. That sends a message to potential customers that the professionals aren't just using TaylorMade clubs because they've been paid endorsement money to do so; rather, this equipment, adopted by the pros as the tools they use to put food on the table, is simply the best available. This commitment, and the results the professionals enjoy, together allow TMaG to say with factual basis and authority something no other manufacturer can say, on TV and in print media: "TaylorMade, the #1 Driver on Tour" (as measured by the Darrell Survey, the industry benchmark for golf club preference on all major professional tours).

Having these goals, both broad in scope but specific in aim, gives TaylorMade a ruler by which to measure all new product designs and marketing initiatives. As appealing as some new direction might be, if it doesn't fit the company's brand statement, it isn't pursued. The attitude is, That idea might be viable, but it isn't for us; it doesn't fit our brand-strategy commitment. As a TaylorMade team member, you know up front that you are going to build performance clubs, golf balls, shoes, and apparel for accomplished golfers and those passionate ones on a steep learning curve, and the product will be validated by the best players in the world. Full stop.

As the TaylorMade team models the company's authentic passion for the game of golf, starting with the CEO and continuing throughout the company, this guiding principle has become not only the strategy of TMaG but also its living culture. And because the culture has become largely self-governing over time—you don't get hired at TMaG unless you already embody it—the company exhibits an almost superhuman alignment between management and workers, company and customers, suppliers and retailers. That in turn frees senior management, including Mark King, to devote their energies to marketing and fine-tuning the company, rather than wasting time getting everyone on the same page. There is only one page at TaylorMade Golf.

For a leader, that's a nice place to be.

The Process: Inclusive and Collaborative

As stated, *leading strategy* is a *process* competency. Thus the leverage for leaders is in designing, creating, and blessing the planning *process*. The process must include the best people and the best ideas, from both within and outside the company, and must foster collaborative thinking and constructive, rigorous discussion. As is true for any effective process, there is a team that owns and runs the process. To accomplish this, a critical first step is deciding who is on the planning team. The composition of players on the team will have much to do with the shape of the plan. Who are the best people to have in the room? One clue: it usually isn't just a top-down organizational chart roster. There are always people in other parts of the company, sometimes at substantially lower levels, who have the needed creativity or orthogonal thinking gene—and they should participate. It is important to have a bottom-up process for gathering ideas from a wide range of people before a plan is made.

The challenge for the leader of a planning process is to support these contributors in a collaborative conversation that distills a wide range of ideas into a workable list of principles from which a real plan can be built. It is simply impossible for a single individual, no matter how brilliant, to understand all of the nuances of the current situation or come up with all of the possible future scenarios. But even if that person could, good leadership demands that all of the requisite players contribute to the process and buy in to its results.

Another substantial challenge is to combine the financial with the strategic—the quantitative results that validate and prove the company is winning the game, and the qualitative accomplishments that position the organization for future success. Both must be allocated resources, including management attention. Ideally, the planning process includes both of these domains of action. The following is an example of a company that has integrated these very different and sometimes competitive activities.

Winnowing Out a Plan

Every leader has his or her mentor, someone who early on showed the potential leader the ropes, or granted responsibility, then monitored the protégé's performance or, later on, provided an example of how to deal with an unusual challenge. So when Tom Carlsen found himself at PowerStar, a storage company serving enterprise customers with high-reliability computer system backup solutions—a business he did not know, but believed he could learn—he cast back over his own career for examples of bosses who had faced a similar challenge.

He didn't have to look far. His mentor, Ed Barker, had come to his last company, an internet commerce business, from previous roles in senior management at software design and computer hardware companies. Tom asked himself, "What had Barker done then to fit into his new company—specifically, to lead the planning process as a newcomer with no credibility in the business?" For one thing, he had hired Tom, who knew the business.

Just as important, Tom remembered, Barker had said, "Listen, I don't need to know enough to design this company's new strategy—I just need to know the people who do know enough to do so and then effectively manage the process." And that's just what he had done.

Now Carlsen found himself in a similar predicament, though in reverse: he was an internet executive who found himself running a storage company.

So Tom took a cue from Barker. He began to develop Power-Star's new business strategy by starting with a bottom-up process by which he solicited ideas for the company to explore or continue in the coming year or two. Of all of these ideas, Tom and his team winnowed out the best fifty, then organized them into ten distinct idea clusters, which they entitled "strategic imperatives."

Then Tom gathered twenty of his top managers in a conference room, and over the course of two days, they built two plans: a financial plan for that year and a plan that included these ten strategic imperatives that would span three years, including the twelve months in front of them. As they began the process, Carlsen made only three demands for the plans: when finished, they had to have *accountability, alignment,* and *autonomy.* Going into more detail, they had to be plans that people could be held accountable to; they had to have the required resources committed to them; and they had to be plans that people could own—that they could be given responsibility for and be able to execute.

And at the end of this process, Tom had the details of the two plans transferred to a giant whiteboard on the side wall of the room, then—and this is important—had all twenty people sign the board with their name. This act of commitment served to remind everyone that by taking that pen and putting their signature on the board, they indeed were the owners of the plan.

Why two plans? Because one is an operating plan, designed solely to meet the quantitative financial quarter-to-quarter expectations of stakeholders, and the other is a strategic plan, designed primarily to advance the position of the company in its industry—to allow it to grow and become more valuable, relevant, and powerful each year. Each strategic imperative has a set of performance metrics, an owner or team of owners, and a set of goals that represent "winning" in that specific area of focus. As a group, these ten strategic imperatives establish a broad and bold commitment to leadership in their marketplace. And a company, or indeed almost any organization, is almost always a tale of two games at the same time: (1) the hard, measurable results, usually financial, that satisfy the shareholders and investors, and (2) the accomplishments born of strategic thinking that position the company or organization for financial success in the years to come. Both are important, both take time and resources, and neither should dominate the other in the minds of senior management—they must maintain a balanced focus on both areas to ensure both short-term and long-term success.

Just as important, in undertaking this process, Tom had also negotiated the usually tricky task (especially for a new CEO) of getting large groups in the company to work together cross-functionally to achieve, if not perfect agreement, at least a solid alignment on common goals. Teamwork, at that level, is a real act of leadership.

Last but not least, Tom was clever enough to know that he was in the difficult position of being both the guy in charge and, for this year, the person in the room least knowledgeable about the company's business. It was therefore incumbent on him to be an enthusiastic participant in the planning process: driving participation, inspiring the best ideas from others, debating proposals along with everyone else, but also staying sufficiently nebulous and reserved so that none of his comments were taken as gospel by his subordinates and ratified by them to score points with the new boss. Needless to say, it was a tightrope walk for Tom. But that's what leaders do—and that's why CEOs earn their pay.

The Plan: Realistic and Compelling

One of the common dangers in planning is—for fear of missing an opportunity (or not defending against a threat)—allowing the process to build too much complexity into the final plan. The liability of complexity, even if it makes the plan seem more complete and elegant, is that it can lead to confusion and difficulties in coordination. It can also take limited resources away from the highest-priority sections of the base plan and spread them too thin across too many possibilities.

Ensuring that a plan is complete and powerful but not overdone comes down to a series of smart and courageous decisions by you, the leader. Your role in the planning process begins with setting the vision and assembling the planning team. After that, unfortunately, many leaders tend to walk away and focus on other pressing matters—with the understandable intention of granting the team sufficient autonomy and latitude—and to return only when the team presents a finished plan.

That is a mistake. As leader, you need to be engaged throughout the process; not to try to influence the contents of the final plan, but to make sure the process moves along with appropriate energy and that the team remains realistic in terms of time, resources, and goals. That means you must set boundary conditions, based on your own appraisal of the people, money, attention, and time available. Those boundaries become increasingly important as you approach the finish line. When you reach the final plan, what is delivered to you for ratification should be a plan to win, but with the widest possible range of scenarios within the constraints of your resources.

All great plans ultimately have great *utility*. And for that to happen, the plan must have the full commitment of everyone involved in their execution. That commitment may begin at the top, with you—but it must be made manifest throughout the organization. That will happen only if all the participants feels that they've had a stake, no matter how small, in that plan's creation.

Great plans are essentially carefully crafted scenarios for victory—and they always balance the conviction of commitment with the reality of the unknown. Though perfect precision is impossible with any plan, good ones always make an effort to account for likely contingencies—the "known unknowns."

A final and equally important task of the leader during planning is leading the team by example, resolving disputes, and breaking logjams. The leader also needs to inspire and motivate creativity when the team is being too careful. When the plan is completed, the leader needs to scrutinize it based on his or her own experiences, then formally and publicly bless it. This adoption process may seem a foregone conclusion if the leader has been intimately involved in the process all along, but in fact, like many rituals, this establishes a highly visible break between the creation of the plan and its execution. It also formally recognizes that all of the players involved share ownership in the plan—and that the leader has made a full commitment to the plan's implementation.

A Good-Looking Plan

- Is clear, complete, and as simple as it can be—team members may be wrong, but they aren't confused.

- Is compelling—a plan to win, with the definition of winning created by and agreed to by the team; a plan that enrolls the team with energy and confidence. It is even OK if everyone is excited about the plan.

- Is committed, and aligns goals, structure, and resources. Members can disagree on *how* to get there, but not on *where* they are going; the plan forces attention and investment to the highest priorities.

- Outlines what the organization *will* do and what it *won't* do—saying "no" is liberating, but the priorities chosen must be reinforced, especially if there are pet projects with passionate owners that were cancelled or postponed.

- Is leveraged—should create competitive advantage and produce nonlinear results.

- Serves customers' needs and anticipates changing external forces—the team needs to skate to where the puck will be, not to where it is today. A good plan positions the

(continued)

company in its sweet spot—the juiciest portion of its
market opportunity.

- Guides and references the organization's actions and
  view of new opportunities—how can the team "stay on
  plan" if it doesn't have one? Any idea should hold up to
  being judged against the principles of the plan.

But at the same time they invest in building the best plan possible, leaders know that, as the saying goes, no plan survives
contact with the enemy—so they must regularly monitor the conditions on the field and remain
flexible enough to revise or even
replace the plan if necessary. Needless to say, in preparation for that
likelihood, it is prudent to never
fall in love with a plan—no matter
how brilliant, no matter whose
idea—because it may have to be
abandoned without a backward glance. The greatest enemy of
strategy is inertia. Almost everyone resists change, and the sta-
tionary weight of the existing set of commitments is substantial.

> "I had a plan, then I got
> hit."
>
> —Joe Louis, boxer

"Houston, We Have a Problem"

You've spent all of that time and energy constructing a great plan.
And it really *is* a great plan—everyone says so. And you've spent all
of that emotional capital getting your people to ratify that plan and
get fully behind it. Most of all, you've abandoned all of the other
competing plans in order to focus on this one—investing precious
time and treasure to prepare for its launch.

Now, to your surprise and disappointment, something's gone
terribly wrong. An unexpected event, a change in the conditions

on which you based your plan, an unanticipated savvy move by your opponent or competitor, and suddenly—reminiscent of the explosion on the *Apollo 13* spacecraft that riveted the world's attention in 1970—your entire plan is threatened.

What do you do now?

It's easy to say "Just change the plan." Nice idea, but in practice it's a whole lot harder to do so. Why is it so hard to abandon or modify a failing plan and quickly devise and implement a new *strategy*? I think there are four logical reasons why changing the plan is difficult—here they are, with the thinking behind each of them.

• *Commitment:* The whole point of leadership is to commit yourself body and soul to the plan, isn't it? Isn't that what you expect and demand from the rest of your team? And it was originally your vision, too—so your entire reputation also rests on the execution of this plan. Besides, doesn't history present endless examples of leaders who had the perfect plan, but then panicked at the first push back and failed? You're supposed to be cool under fire—so why react prematurely?

• *Confusion:* How do you really know the threat or situation is as bad as it is being portrayed? There is the "fog of war," after all—so perhaps the people sending you these reports are working from inaccurate or limited information. Maybe it is they who are panicking. Besides, it's you who has the Big Picture, so if anyone would be first to identify a problem, it would be you.

• *Complexity:* Your team has spent an enormous amount of time devising your plan. Every eventuality (well, *almost* every, it appears) has been covered, duties assigned, resources transferred, and precise timetable developed. Now are you going to throw all of that—or at least a lot of it—out because things aren't going quite the way you expected them to? Please. Now that you are in the thick of things, where are you going to find the time and resources for a new and revised plan? Better to make a few small revisions and stick with what you've got. After all, who says that the situation won't turn back in your favor?

- *Communications:* The plan is already under way. The troops are in the field. And you spend a lot of time training them and getting them ready to perform at the highest productivity level. In the process you even began to change the culture of the organization to more precisely align it with the nature of your plan. Are you really going to change everything now based on what might be a trifle? How are you even going to reach all of those people? And even if you could call them back, what would you tell them? Are you really going to retrain them? There's no time! Are you going to transform your culture *again*? On the fly?

In other words, there are an endless number of excuses and reasons not to abandon your plan and develop a new strategy. But there is one overriding reason to do so: if you don't adapt and change, *you are going to lose*.

As a leader, your primary job is to lead your team to success. And any risk that you allow to reduce the chances of that success counts as a failure on your part. In other words, it doesn't matter how much time, energy, and money was spent on developing the original plan; how much time you spent training the team; the status of your reputation. All of that is now sunk cost, and what matters now is whether or not the plan is working. If it isn't, all that matters is the *new* strategy that you now create and implement ASAP to replace it.

What about the matter of incomplete knowledge? How can you be sure those early reports of failure are really true? You can't, at least not 100 percent. But that's why it's so crucial to create strong two-way communication with your team in those early stages. Because now is when you are really going to need it: the knowledge that your team is going to be honest with themselves, the data, and you; their willingness to trust your judgment even when it changes; and their ability to move quickly in concert. And you can further improve your odds by using that same apparatus to quickly gather any information you can to confirm your suspicions.

But then what? Suppose your worst fears come true and your current plan is driving you toward failure? Do you really have the time and resources to come up with a new strategy? The answer is: *you have no choice*. You do your best with what you've got, and you use the least possible amount of time to do so.

The good news is that what you've got may be considerable. You've built a great team, you've put in place a powerful and supple communications network, and it may turn out that a lot of the original plan is still applicable. Remember, these are the moments when having built leadership credibility and trust with your team will pay you back in spades. This is the time to leverage every ounce of goodwill that you've established and to call your troops to the front of the battle.

The key is to stay cool, be unsentimental and untied to the past, and most of all, be decisive. It is in moments like this that you earn your pay as a leader. Find that right strategy, find it fast, and get to work executing it.

Stickiness

The ability to change a committed strategy in the face of a threat to its success is clearly, 100 percent a matter of decisive, thoughtful, bold leadership. But, there are times when the other side of courage is needed—the ability to stick with a strategy even when it looks suspect, if you believe in it deeply. Maybe a sign of a great leader is, as Kenny Rogers sings, to "know when to hold 'em, know when to fold 'em." Here's a case in which staying the course was the right thing to do. As in earlier stories, the names have been changed to protect the innocent.

DLT, a venture-funded enterprise resource planning (ERP) software company, had committed itself to what is called a "bowling alley" business strategy, in the familiar vernacular of Geoff Moore's *Crossing the Chasm*—the informal "bible" that most tech companies use to build their go-to-market plans. It's called "bowling alley" because the idea is that if you can knock down the lead pin—by dominating a specific application solution in a specific target market—you can knock down additional pins by moving to a new segment with the same solution or to a new solution in the same segment. This strategy requires discipline and commitment by the entire sales and marketing team to be successful.

All the stakeholders at DLT had signed up for this plan. The industry DLT had picked as its lead bowling pin was the big domestic insurance companies. And the unspoken rule of this strategy was this: *Whatever the Big Insurance market wants, we'll deliver it. If the market's not insurance, they'll have to buy what we've already got.* In other words, all of the company's R&D research money was targeted at making products with the features the big insurance providers needed; if other target markets wanted product, it would have to be the standard, existing feature set.

It worked brilliantly. In 1992, DLT had revenues of $4 million; a year later it forecast $12 million. Everything was going precisely as planned, and all based on 100-percent commitment to the single vertical market, with a solution custom tailored to meet this vertical segment's needs in the ERP area.

But then the sales guys started acting like good sales guys and digging up business. One of them located, through a series of unplanned events, a $1.5 million new customer opportunity in the pharmaceutical industry—and all it would take to close the deal was a few new custom features in the product. This pharma company really wanted the DLT software and lobbied persuasively in an attempt to convince the DLT engineering team to modify the code. Needless to say, none of these new features would be of any interest to Big Insurance—they were specific to the peculiarities of drug development.

Lee Harris, the CEO of DLT, always knew that there would be "the deal" that would test the company's commitment to its bowling alley vertical market strategy—and now that the moment had come. He resolved to use this opportunity to make a statement.

The sales team asked for a meeting to debate the merits of this potential deal, and Harris agreed. There, the salespeople argued passionately for the order. Not surprising, in a company DLT's size, with a sales force of just eight people, the pharma deal represented one salesman's entire yearly quota.

In the end—after a lot of debate, hand wringing, tears, and grief—Harris held fast: there would be no special programs for the pharmaceutical industry. This decision was his, and the buck stopped at his desk. He would later say that turning down a million-dollar-plus deal against an eight-million-dollar plan was one of the hardest things he ever had to do.

But Harris was right. He realized that the decision wasn't about hitting the revenue numbers, but about the company's commitment to the integrity of its strategy. He could have justified going after the pharmaceutical business with that "no plan ever survives contact with the enemy" saying. But that would have been a rationalization: adjusting on the fly to the changing conditions of the insurance market is very different from abandoning that market in an opportunistic pursuit of some quick money in another—a move that would have compromised the company's planning for years to come.

As you might guess, the sales team was furious. *We're a young company,* they told Harris, *we ought to be more flexible.* They accused him of still having big company thinking and being unable to adapt to life in a start-up. *Besides,* they told him, *the new engineering requirements aren't that difficult, we can pull them off with almost no impact on our insurance business.*

But what Harris saw was a young company that was already becoming distracted by easy money; that was already saying to the world: we can't walk the talk. What would it signal, Harris asked, if DLT were to do this—other than that we aren't committed, we really haven't "burned our boats" with our stated strategy, we allow others to determine our destiny, and, finally, *we aren't serious*. He hung tough with his decision.

Later, Harris would joke that one of the phrases he came up with during this experience was: *We may not be right, but at least we aren't confused.* Even if his people didn't yet understand, Harris had learned the most important lesson about strategy: it is not enough to design it, or even to align your organization around it—what counts is whether you are serious about making a full commitment to it, and not wavering until a real threat of failure looms.

This real-life story ends well. DLT came to dominate ERP in the insurance industry, with an over 70-percent market share; it expanded into other logical vertical markets over time, grew to over $200 million in revenue in the following five years, and ultimately went public with a billion-dollar market cap. Harris's tough but principled call may have provided just the focus they needed to become a significant force in the ERP software world.

Granted, no book can describe the exact criteria for when to stick and when to change, and honest mistakes will be made in times when the situation cannot be fully known. The main point here is that leaders lead, and this will be your call, and you have to make the best decision you can at the moment of truth. And that's all you can do. Just remember that no one else will make these decisions and rally the resources in a new direction, or have them stay the course—this is the work of leaders.

The Essentials of Leading Strategy

- Strategy is a process competency. The output of the process is plan. The data that informs that plan should come from the best sources you can find, including bottom-up ideas. No ego or hierarchy or pride of authorship. A complete meritocracy is the best model for great ideas.

- The best plans are made from accurate, unbiased, clean data, and outside-of-the-box creative thinking.

- Beware of letting your authority unintentionally discourage input from lower levels. Few will compete with the boss's ideas, especially the ideas they think the boss loves.

- Make sure the plan is a plan to win. Ownership is key to commitment, and healthy debate allows the team to air their differences, commit to the best ideas, and align on a shared view of the plan.

- Strategy establishes priorities—the things we will do and the things we will not do. It also allocates and commits resources. A plan without committed resources is merely a good intention.

- A great strategy is clear, simple, and easy to socialize. Everyone in the organization should know and be able to articulate the high points of the plan.

CHAPTER SIX

LEADING EXECUTION
Action to Results

Leadership is the art of getting someone else to do
something you want done because he wants to do it.
                                    —*Dwight Eisenhower*

Men make history and not the other way around.
In periods where there is no leadership, society
stands still. Progress occurs when courageous,
skillful leaders seize the opportunity to change
things for the better.
                                    —*Harry S. Truman*

Execution is about results. At the end of the day, leaders are held
accountable; they get paid to produce the agreed-upon results.
To believe anything else is to kid yourself and to court failure.

Execution is where the rubber meets the road, the snap is taken,
the play is run, and the shot is hit. There is no score until the game
starts. At that moment, preparation yields to the event itself, and
winners and losers are determined. There is no place to hide.

That isn't to say that execution stands entirely alone (this fact
is forgotten by many leaders). In most organizations, every day's a
game day; in fact, most days are—from the staging of the next

action, to the ongoing recruiting of the right talent, to the hurried training that takes place on the sidelines based on new moves by the competition that have just been spotted.

Most of all, the strategy process is still active long after execution has been initiated—in fact, it can't even truly begin until that moment, when the *plan* is at last tested by the reality of the field of play.

A simple metaphor to illuminate the relationships among people, strategy, and execution is to consider the process of building a new custom home. There are handfuls of people—the architects, builders, homeowner, and myriad experts and consultants in lots of related disciplines—who form the team embarking on such a project. Their collective input, often led by the architect who serves as process manager for the strategy, is converted to a set of plans—a big roll of blueprints that represent the aligned interests of all the parties. This is the agreement about what is going to be built and, substantially, how it all will happen. It includes the desired outcomes of all the parties and reveals most of the methodology to be used in building the house. It is a strategy for the home—the plans for the builders to get started, plus any other contextual information that will help prepare the construction team for potential problems or special situations along the way. Before the first footing is poured or the first board is cut, the plan to achieve the goals has been signed. This plan cannot account for all the possible unforeseen challenges or changes, but it is, as written, a plan to win. From there, the action can begin—hammers swinging, concrete pouring, windows and doors getting framed in, and all the rest. All according to plan.

With this metaphor as a backdrop, we can see that there is something special about execution that is distinct from all of the other Nine Essentials of Unusually Excellent leadership. It is not about hiring or developing the team. It is not about getting plans into place. *It is about taking action.* There is an energy and a pace, and certainly a competitiveness, to getting things done. It is the thrill of the game.

The first two factors that make execution distinct from the domains of people and strategy are *measurement* and *feedback*. Planning is the province of statistics and probabilities: What is our market size? How well does this player hit against lefties? What are the chances that this plan will work? In contrast, as we put the game into play, we start to get feedback from the actions we take, and we begin to get some measurement of progress. Execution, however, lives on the actual performance data coming in: What's the score? How are we doing in the Japanese market? How do bookings compare to billings?

The other significant feature that distinguishes execution from the other steps is the presence of time—the game *clock*. There are the performance and production timeframes built into the calendar—the week, the month, the quarter, and the fiscal year. Other leadership processes have their own internal clocks, but none are so driven by external deadlines as execution. Planning, of course, has its own deadlines, but they are rarely precise and the consequences are usually not fatal. By comparison, miss a product introduction date—as Microsoft did (by nearly two years!) with its Vista operating system—and the entire enterprise (or in the case of Vista, the personal computer industry) can be nearly wrecked. However, there are many examples in which the pressure of deadlines has extracted extraordinary performances from ordinary teams or people. Most accomplishments that had a "mission impossible" challenge were characterized that way, in part, because of an unreasonable time frame associated with the project or objective. The SAT test is timed—and limited to exactly four hours—for a reason: we want to know not just how smart people are, but also how they perform under the pressure of a deadline.

Solve the Hard Problems First

To highlight the nature of execution, and to understand the supreme importance of urgency, I reflect on a story I heard from Reid Hoffman, cofounder of PayPal and now chairman of LinkedIn, who compares the reality of being an entrepreneur to jumping off a high cliff and needing to build an airplane before you hit the ground. This analogy clearly highlights both the importance of solving the mission-critical problems first, and the merciless nature of the time clock running out before you get it all done. In this metaphor you'd have no illusion that you'd need to get the fuselage, engines, and wings put together first, and learn quickly if there were any insurmountable problems with those *essential* items required for success. You'd identify the points of failure early. And you'd demand the feedback and measurements that reveal progress on getting those critical items behind you. You would have no incentive to amuse or distract yourself with second-tier tasks until you were sure you had a basic, workable design—a winning plan.

This brings to mind the pervasive and dangerous "majoring in the minors" syndrome, wherein very talented people can lose focus on the critical path problems that must be solved to transform an idea into reality. Those are often the knottiest problems, and sometimes we resist them for a period of time, preferring to create some satisfying momentum on simpler tasks, or ones that are simply more fun. Leaders must develop an eye and ear for this weakness—and must try to listen for it in every conversation and look for it in every ops review. They must relentlessly redirect energy to the hard problems, realizing that it is human nature to drift from the tough stuff in favor of more emotionally fulfilling and easier project modules. Finally, returning to Reid's cliff and airplane metaphor, the impending collision with the ground is your reminder that time—or money—can eventually run out before you get it done, and it is then, quite simply, game over.

Those two factors—measurement plus feedback, and timing—combined with the win-or-lose imperative transform leading execution into a role that is one part battlefield commander, one part navigator, and one part cheerleader:

Battlefield commander, because there are times when you must
lead from the front, setting an example of measured

urgency that doesn't tip over into hysteria. You must provide energy to create momentum, but do so with a steady hand. You must display a soldier's toughness and be willing to take a punch from the enemy.

Navigator, because leading an organization during its execution phase is largely one of monitoring incoming feedback data and field results and then reformulating strategy on the fly to best respond to these changes. As navigator, you must provide advice that helps your troops adapt, knowing that your voice carries more influence than others. It is highly unlikely that others will see—or have the courage to voice—the changes to course and speed that you will have to implement.

Cheerleader, because you have to keep your people in the game—continuously motivating them, getting them the support they need, lifting their morale when things go bad, and tempering their enthusiasm to keep them focused on victory. Most of all, you have to instill a will to win amongst all of the stakeholders in the initiative. In the inevitable dark moments—when everyone is tired and the game seems to be no fun, or when serious fatigues sets in—your team will count on you to keep the faith, the spirit, and the energy. This obligation comes with the title of *leader*.

The reality is that leading execution is a $7 \times 24 \times 365$ project. In most businesses, there is no time-out for a commercial. We live in an always-on, completely connected world. In the new global economy, leadership means being on the field every day, sometimes all day, and in many or all time zones worldwide. Even when you take your team off the field for the occasional off-site planning meeting, the game goes on—and you must be able to send the troops back into battle with a conviction to make up lost time or hold the lead.

As the leader of the execution phase, your work never ends. Even as you are called to command, navigate, or coach the action, you must also be recruiting, training, and deploying new talent; extending and broadening your external network of relationships; maintaining communication with all your key constituents, looking for new sources of feedback and insight; and constantly keeping a weather eye for an unexpected change in the competitive environment.

This part of leading—the high-stakes, play-to-win execution game—is enthralling, enriching and intellectually engaging, but it is also exhausting, which is why your final challenge as the senior leader of execution is to pace yourself, carefully pick your battles, and, at all costs, avoid burnout. Adrenaline will sustain you for a surprisingly long time, at high levels, but eventually even that drug will lose its effectivity. You have to establish and guard the work/life boundaries that allow you to regroup, reflect, and recharge. You need to be at your best, as often as humanly possible. You must learn to truly delegate to strong subordinates and let them fully manage their accountabilities, using check-ins and metrics to guide their actions. As romantic (and liberating) as martyrdom to your team may sound, it is also a betrayal: that commitment you made to your team at the beginning was for the duration, to celebrate victory with them one day—and they expect that.

At the Edges

As scientists and engineers know, one of the best ways to understand the average of anything is to study the extreme conditions. The median or mean can show you only so much; for the rest you need to explore several deviations out, where the stresses are greatest and the consequences of failure most severe.

To gain another perspective on the leadership of execution, we can make the same journey of discovery—out into the world of so-called high-reliability organizations (HROs): SWAT teams, emergency rooms, air traffic control, and the like. For HROs, precision in execution is literally a matter of life and death. Precision in recruiting, training, planning, communication, coordination—and most of all, timing. Even precision in *language*: imagine the precise choice of words necessary for an ambulance driver to call in to an emergency room about a patient on the way, or the "shoot" order given by a SWAT team commander to one of its snipers. Precision, especially with regard to communication, is a top-down principle— it doesn't happen in the middle or lower portions of an organization, unless it is modeled at the top, consistently and passionately.

This is a model of *zero tolerance* team execution, where even the slightest error, even imprecision, can be fatal. So how do these HROs learn to operate with this level of accuracy? There are six components:

- *Reliable communications and information processes:* You can start by putting together a strong communications infrastructure. Make sure all the equipment and information is supplied, so that everyone knows how to reach the parties of importance to do their jobs. "I couldn't reach you" is not an excuse in an HRO. You also need to be sure that the data available to and transmitted by this network is both accurate and comprehensible. This increases speed and reduces error—especially if, in your training, you've made certain that every team member knows the nomenclature, code words, and jargon by heart. Just as important, you need to lead by example: you cannot expect your subordinates to remain in regular and reliable communication with each other if you, by comparison, choose to remain above the fray.

- *Continuous training and apprenticeships:* Not just certification in each of the requisite skills for the job—though that is certainly a large part of it—but simulations of all likely scenarios. That's why SWAT teams have sophisticated practice facilities, and why each member must regularly requalify on equipment. It's why EMT professionals not only must be qualified on all of the emergency equipment on the vehicle but also undergo long hours of practice on dummies and real patients. Each of these HRO careers has a well-established trajectory that begins with a period of apprenticeship in which the trainee is teamed with a veteran who oversees the apprentice in action and can provide advice and backup in real time.

- *Standardize and synchronize:* In the world of HROs, almost every process has been standardized and codified to the highest possible degree. Every word an air traffic controller says to a pilot in the air has a precise and predetermined meaning and has been tested for clarity over microwave transmission. SWAT team members practice thousands of times the exact placement of their feet, trigger fingers, eye placement to the rifle scope, proximity to other team members, and so on. For a fireman or EMT, every piece of equipment on their vehicle is always stored in exactly the same place and in exactly the same way—so that they don't have to think twice about where to find it or put it to use. Why so much detail? Because removing any confusion from the basic operation not only reduces the chance of error but also frees up time to focus on more complex and less likely scenarios.

As for synchronizing, ever watch a fire crew respond to a medical emergency, or a SWAT team enter a building, or air traffic controllers manage a dozen or more planes in a single airspace? Everybody not only plays his or her own part but also recognizes that each is part of a much larger *field* of activity in which they all must coordinate with each other's work. That's why they've been trained to simultaneously focus on the task before them while also remaining cognizant of the actions of all of the other team members—a task made much easier if they don't have to think about their equipment, their role, or what they are expected to do next.

- *Mission-goal clarity and loyalty:* It all starts with the notion that everyone in the organization shares the value of doing a job correctly. This is followed by a crystal-clear understanding of the goals. Loyalty to team members, the mission, and the goals is paramount. Time matters, and the stakes are high; and there is great satisfaction in getting the job done—accomplishing the goal, as a team. There is no attention on any individual's ego needs. When you have a skier down, or a car in a ditch, or a hostage situation, the stakes are high, and it clears the mind of all petty concerns and distractions.

• *Empower the front line:* No one can micromanage during a high-intensity situation. These are the times when leaders have to let decisions come from the lowest level possible. The best decisions happen at the level of expertise necessary for the moment. In times of crisis, a rigid hierarchy can be fatal. Official rank becomes irrelevant. The investments made in training pay off here, when the employees closest to the action—or the customer—can confidently and competently resolve problems without escalating the issue to their bosses, which would waste precious time and resources.

• *Redundancy:* A second aspect of the apprenticeship-veteran relationship mentioned earlier is that all tasks have at least two parties involved to spot each other's errors, provide backup in case one party is not in a position to function, and offer a second perspective on a judgment call. This redundancy is also useful during the feedback process to fill in blanks and provide a second set of eyes.

To this list I would add one more factor, which doesn't quite fit with the others but is no less important: *passion.* You don't take these jobs—and you certainly don't keep them—unless you love them and you also have the stomach for the pressure and a thirst for the action. People who are attracted to these HRO occupations embrace—even thrive on—the social importance of their work, the high-stakes nature of the outcomes, and the meaningful, sometimes life-saving results. Michael Jordan once said, "With thirty seconds left in the game, some people want to watch, some people want to pass, some people want to shoot the ball. We want the people who want to shoot." It takes a certain personality and attitude to consistently play under the pressure of high expectations. And it takes someone who is also prepared to follow orders instantly and work as part of a team, yet still retain his or her individuality and ability to see things differently from everyone else. You should try to find these people, not make them—I haven't seen many people who acquire this mind-set along their career path. This is a personality type, not an aspiration.

What can leaders of ordinary (non-HRO) organizations learn from HROs? Almost everything. Those six (plus one) factors can teach leaders of ordinary organizations a great deal about the basics of disciplined execution. The stakes may not be quite as high (sloppiness may not equal death, although it could mean ruin), and the timing not quite so precise, but in every other way your goals should reflect the best practices of HROs as much as possible. You should exhibit in yourself, and recruit for the team around you, an enthusiasm for risk, competition, and pressure. You should empower the front line to decide and act on everything they reasonably can. Whether you are introducing a new product, entering a new market, or embarking on a new initiative, you should standardize routine operations—messaging, sales and marketing materials, presentations, and so on—as much as possible. Then you must train heavily toward those standards, so that their contents become second nature. You can also use HROs as a reminder, when your team starts to whine a bit or moan about it all being "too hard." HRO people can't and don't complain—they just get it done.

Most execution strategies don't require the kind of synchronization between players needed for, say, managing eighty airliners circling over O'Hare. But tasks still need to take place in sequence, and each step in a critical path must be completed before you move on to the next one. Air traffic controllers coordinate by sharing the same data; SWAT team members do it by well-known commands and highly reliable communications. The combination of HRO factors that you should attempt to implement and model will depend on the specifics of your organization's mission and the circumstances of the playing field. However, there is clearly something to learn from looking at HRO principles; it's an admirable standard to which you may aspire. Try to put one or two of those principles into play in your group as soon as you can.

Leadership Leverage in Execution

Now that we have a model for high-performance, zero-mistakes execution—the HRO—let's highlight the three leverage points for leaders at work in ordinary organizations. Remember, we aren't teaching or modeling execution, we are *leading* it.

First, we need to lead the process and set the standards for the *right goals*. Next, we need to lead the design process to create the *appropriate metrics*. Finally, we need to ensure a *winner's commitment* and make sure that attitude permeates the culture.

Curb Your Enthusiasm: Focus, Commit, and Deliver

You hire your team members, at least in part, for their enthusiasm for the project, and you try to cultivate that enthusiasm in some degree by exhibiting it yourself. Enthusiasm, properly managed, can create a virtuous cycle, whereby team members support one another in an ever-upward spiral of productivity, performance, and, with luck, success.

At first glance, it's hard to imagine enthusiasm having a down side. But it certainly does, and it's called *overcommitment*. Enthusiastic individuals and teams have a tendency to blow right past manageable, predictable gains and focus on Big Wins. They swing from their heels, hoping to hit a home run every time. In doing so, in allowing enthusiasm for its own sake to take hold of a project, they turn it from a valuable asset into a major threat.

Even your most talented people will have a tendency to aim too big, to take on more than they can accomplish, and even take shortcuts to victory. In fact, they are often the most likely people to exhibit this behavior. For the leader it's easy to get caught up in the excitement, to support the shortcutters and to let the enthusiasts realize their ambitions.

But as military leaders are taught over and over, one of the most dangerous times is when victory is in sight and the enemy is fleeing the field. That's when organization can break down, mistakes are made, and defensible lines are stretched. A great rout sometimes turns into a stunning reversal of fortune.

Your job as a leader is to maintain discipline and order right through the moment when success is achieved, maintain coordination and channels of communication, curb your own enthusiasm, and most of all *assure focused execution*. *You can plan a great menu, buy superb ingredients, cook a beautiful meal, but if you*

drop it on the floor on your way from the kitchen to the dining room,
you lose.

A few years back, I wrote a piece for the *Harvard Business Review* entitled "The Five Messages Leaders Must Manage." We'll discuss the overall message of the essay more in Chapter Seven, A Leader's Execution. For now, I want to focus on a brief sidebar I wrote for the article that I'm now convinced may be as important, at least in real-life practice, as the entire rest of the essay.

In this sidebar, I proposed the concept of "84 Great Things." What I meant, in this example of holding a tight focus on goal setting, was that if you, as leader, have seven direct reports and you convince them to complete just three initiatives—all of them important, but also very doable—per quarter, by the end of the year just your immediate subordinates will have completed seven times three times four for a total of eighty-four important projects in support of your strategy.

As a group, these eighty-four completed initiatives would have a profound impact on your team's reaching its bigger goals for the year. And imagine just how much more would be accomplished if those seven subordinates set the same expectations for each of their lieutenants—and so on, all the way down through the organization chart. The enterprise would become unbelievably efficient, surefooted, competent, and accomplished—and competitively unequalled. They would spend an incredible percentage of the total organizational energy on the right things.

Yet for all of this impact, the key is the consistent focus on small, important, and most of all *achievable* milestones that combine in symphonic fashion to produce large-scale success. Tellingly, the biggest threat to a program of eighty-four great things is not falling short of the stated goals, but reaching beyond them in an attempt to overachieve. The real enemy to finishing "84 Great Things" is not the difficulty of the high-priority goals; it is the temptation to work on the eighty-fifth objective (and beyond) before, or at the expense of, the ones you have already committed to. In other words, a tendency to complicate the mission and an unmanaged enthusiasm will drive your team—and perhaps you too—to try to do even more than they signed up for. And that will be the undoing of the huge opportunity that "84 Great Things" represents—which is absolutely completing those eighty-four promised things.

The problem isn't enthusiasm, per se; it's *unbridled* enthusiasm. You want to set goals that are both clearly defined and bounded. In the world of pervasive "big hairy audacious goals" (BHAGs, with a nod to Jim Collins's *Good to Great*), leading the goal-setting process to arrive at objectives that are perfectly sized is very tricky work, but this effort has never been more important to success than in the geographically dispersed, virtual organization. While top performers are inspired by "stretch" goals that seem slightly out of their reach, smart team members will not waste their time training for a "three-minute mile." Goals that are clearly beyond any reasonable confidence of achievement are worse than easy goals—they actually disengage the energy in the team. The predictable and natural response is "Why bother?" Taskmasters and pace-setting leaders need to learn the fine line between an invigorating challenge and a wholly deflating expectation. They also need to realize that everyone on the team may not share their level of maniacal commitment.

You must enforce, again with your own example, the rule of "first things first." There is perhaps no higher leverage discipline than making sure you complete immediate, high-priority goals before running off to take on others. When dealing with high-performing types, you will need to resist their natural ambition to add value to the agreed-to set of goals by wanting to commit to even bigger results. There is already enough complexity in most ambitious goals. Simplifying them is harder. The trick is to reframe success in terms of mastering the fundamentals, producing results, and learning more about the work along the way. As in golf, making more five-foot putts than the rest of the field often wins the tournament even though it is less glamorous than hitting three-hundred-yard drives in the fairway.

One great way to keep team members focused on the task at hand is to begin with the precise enunciation of those goals at the beginning of the quarter, perform regular audits and progress reports during the quarter, and conduct a post-mortem at the end. There is a natural tendency to honor only those team members who occasionally smash home runs; you must not forget to reward those players who reliably punch out singles and doubles and hit for average.

In choosing your challenges as you set objectives, consider the ruling criterion in the fairy tale of Goldilocks and the three bears. Goals should be neither too big nor too small, too difficult nor too easy—they should be *just right*. One of the highest-leverage opportunities for you as a leader is to identify that sweet spot and assure yourself that the organization has committed to achieving the optimal set of objectives for the business or mission at hand.

It Isn't Real If You Don't Measure It

Performance metrics are the conscience of execution—they keep you grounded and honest in the face of the confusion and pressure of driving the action and results toward the expectations that have been set for you and your team. They are not emotional—they just tell you the facts of how you are doing. They aren't subject to disappointment. They just report status. They are mostly just numbers, with no interpretation—that is for humans to provide. For you as a leader, they are friend, confidant, and assistant manager. Done right, metrics simulate a full-time performance manager, directing massive amounts of resources toward the high-priority goals.

Measuring what matters is an extremely high-leverage opportunity. As with hiring, most Unusually Excellent leaders are heavily involved in the design process for the dashboards and key performance indicators that will be used to track progress and critical stats. The right metrics will serve you in enormously useful ways; a wrong or incomplete set of indicators, like a malfunctioning airplane cockpit, will spell failure—perhaps not immediately, but inevitably. This is a top-down activity that is worth getting right.

Metrics are always logically linked to the goals to which you have committed in the transition from the strategy output of a plan to the dedicated action of execution. There is no sense asking the question "How are we doing?" without a reference to a goal. My smart-ass answer to that question would be "Compared to what?" My VP, engineering at Whistle Communications, Doug Brent, would remind me: "I can't tell you if something is good or bad, unless you tell me the goal. It all depends on the goal."

In most management by objectives (MBO) programs, an "as measured by" (AMB) or a key performance indicator (KPI) statement will be part of the syntax. So the structure of most goals as written includes a measureable goal, a time frame, and the measurement proposed to track it.

"We'll do <u>what</u> by <u>when</u>, (as measured by) _____."

For example: <u>sell twelve new airplanes</u> by <u>October 1, 2011</u>, (as measured by) <u>signed contracts with prices and delivery schedules by customers.</u>

Again referencing the organizations that work with BHAGs, it is more difficult to measure success in the short run because the end goals is almost always unreasonable, by definition. BHAGs are designed to inspire results that would surpass those in an ordinary organization where attainable goals—or even stretch goals—are the norm. However, as Matt McCauly, CEO of Gymboree reminded me:

> In a world of BHAGs, you must have interim goals that measure *progress*. We figure out what level of progress we want, by when, and measure against that, in line with eventually achieving our BHAGs. If you define success as reaching the Big Goal in a black and white fashion, no one would want to play. They would always commit to a goal they can reach. Most of the time, 80 percent of the way to an outrageous goal

is a bigger accomplishment than overachieving on a smaller vision of success.

We measure everything we possibly can in financial terms. If we can't distill it to a result measured in dollars, we wonder if it is really a goal. Even seemingly qualitative goals—like customer satisfaction—can be tracked in a way that ultimately results in a financial result. This builds a culture that remembers that, at the end of the day, we post financial results, and while we are working to improve everything we can, we focus on tying our actions to driving shareholder value.

The real discipline in metrics is to measure the *hard stuff*. What is the hard stuff? It is the feedback from the live action on the field that reveals and illuminates progress of the factors most closely aligned with the critical assumptions of the project, like early sales performance and quality or cost feedback—those critical elements for which we have our fingers crossed, hoping they go well, because if they don't, the project may suddenly be at risk. Special attention must be paid to the factors that can warn us, early on, if serious danger is lurking. We all get attached to our ideas, and we don't really want to see—at least not early in the game—that we may have whiffed the whole concept. We know from statistics that for every new commercial food product that hits the shelves in your local supermarket, eight others have failed, and if one of those was your baby, it would have been hard to hear and accept the focus group feedback or the early sales numbers that showed it was doomed to failure. However, the organizations with the collective emotional strength to stomach those tough, early-in-the-game numbers can learn to adapt and change quickly when things aren't working. Only with the right data can we save time and money by early course correction. Interpretation and judgment are a big part of the decision to change direction, but those decisions can be made intelligently only with good data. (More on this in Chapter Eight, A Leader's Decision Making.)

Another ethic to instill in the metrics process is to determine and measure those factors that correlate very highly with winning. We can and should collect proxy data that, short of showing us the final outcome, will tell us a lot about the probability of winning. On the PGA Tour, myriad statistics are kept, but there are always a couple of key metrics—often it's scoring average and sometimes it's basics like percentage of drives in the fairway or percentage of putts made under ten feet—that have a surprisingly high correlation to the total money list, which is the ultimate measure of success each year. Therefore you'd be silly, or in denial, to measure everything *except* those critical factors, knowing full well that they are your biggest clues to overall success. In every business or organization, there are five to ten key measurements that, if you knew nothing else, would give you a "knee of the curve" (right moment) understanding of your position in the game and your chances of winning. These kind of stats also have an external reference—sometimes industry benchmarks or standards that you do not set or control, but must know, if you are to avoid living in an illusion about what level of performance represents a winning standard in your industry or game. If you want to be an Olympic swimmer, you can easily learn the race times it takes to make the team, or win a medal, within a very small margin of error. There is no confusion about the standard required for success. Most business measurements are very similar—you can know the performance levels that are required. And make sure you measure it exactly as the rest of the world measures it. And make sure that, in learning what the interim metrics look like, you don't confuse an alternate accomplishment with the result you wanted. No results plus a good story is not equal to results. Beware the temptation to be in denial of the numbers you need to win. Ignorance is not bliss.

The topic just discussed leads us to two final points about metrics, and then we'll move on to the opportunity for metrics to help manage behavior. First, remember that when linking internal measurements to the outside world—especially to the known standards or benchmarks it takes to compete and win—there is a tendency to shoot the messenger. I watched a CEO take some real heat at a meeting where she was explaining the basis for the following quarter's sales projections. Granted, they were ambitious goals, and the reaction internally was to resist these objectives—the talk on the team was of how unreasonable they were. The CEO, realizing she was a messenger in the process of being shot, shifted the conversation to remind her team that the competitive outside world, not she, had set this bar for expected performance, and the reality of winning in the marketplace was represented in the numbers she had just shared—like it or not. While the team could certainly commit to something less than the standard required to be relevant, it would be a fool's game, and a short one at that. They would be out of business in two quarters at the revenue level the team hoped for. In that moment, she reframed the context of that conversation—from that of an overly demanding boss to one of *chief communicator*—passing along the knowledge of what it would take to win, referenced to the competitive outside world. Indeed, a favor, not a burden—if winning is the goal.

Finally, beware of making the process of building measurement systems an unofficial Olympic sport within your organization. Remember, the metrics are the menu, not the food. This task should not become a separate competition within the organization. With all due respect to CFOs, they sometimes want to measure everything they can, instead of exactly what is absolutely required, and no more. You don't get paid for having the best dashboard, you get paid for winning, and sometimes more is less. Too much information, or data poorly organized or presented, can serve to confuse and distract the action. Most often, less is more, and the five to ten most important metrics, thoughtfully chosen and rigorously gathered, are all you need. But the choice of those critical measures is one of the most important decisions that leaders make; therefore they must be involved in the design of the scorecard.

Let the Dashboard Drive

Another opportunity that arises from measuring what matters is the chance to use the right metrics as a *management* assistant—helping to naturally direct attention, focus, and commitment to the right activities—which are defined as the ones that we measure, discuss, and pay people to achieve. As conveyed by the "shoot the messenger" example just described, the fact that metrics are unemotional and consistent allows leaders to use them to manage behavior at scale. Management is distinct from leadership because *managing* implies control and accountability—exactly what you want in a goal measurement context. When you have the right metrics in place, an enormous amount of energy will flow toward accomplishing the goals being tracked, and that leaves leaders to do real leadership work, rather than needing to direct behavior to the right activities.

Finally, remember that you can measure almost anything—and what you measure will almost certainly "improve." And as the Crosby Quality Institute reminds us: *You will get what you inspect, not what you expect.* I know one CEO who was constantly entertaining requests from his sales force for changes to the company's product line—change orders—in response to "customer requests." Using customers' needs to drive change is an age-old tactic of savvy salespeople, but in this case very few of these requested changes, which came at great expense in engineering time and cost, resulted in orders from the people who had passionately argued the case. Instead of getting upset about it, the CEO simply asked that the team begin to track the percentage of change orders resulting in sales orders, and—what do you know?—this costly practice came to a screeching halt as soon as the sales force knew their bosses were looking at this data, by salesperson, every month

Measuring what matters is perhaps the very highest use of leadership authority in leading the domain of execution. Once the plan is set, the resources and funding are committed, and the action starts, there is mostly just feedback and response to the unknowns of the battle to be managed. The one thing you must have, to make the real-time course corrections that will inevitably be required, is good data. Invest in the design and the machinery required to gather, analyze, and present the data you need—quickly, accurately, and easily. This, more than anything else, will serve your leadership needs in the arena of live ammo—where the score is kept, and the winners get to keep playing, and the losers go home.

It's Just Like Pinball: If You Win, You Get to Play Again

We now arrive at the third and final point of leader's leverage in *leading execution*—maintaining a *winner's mind-set*.

Execution is about just one thing: *results*. And for any team, the only acceptable result should be *winning*.

That may seem self-evident, obvious, and logical; in fact, if you ask everyone, individually, they will say *of course we are here to win*. You may be saying *the goal is always to win*. In a win-lose situation, nobody wants to lose.

But you'd be amazed how many talented, well-led teams, enterprises, companies, and organizations, many of them with clear, reasonable goals, set out to do just that—and then, inexplicably to the outside observer, veer away. I've seen literally hundreds of instances in which teams, despite all of the right intentions, have failed to win victories that should have been easily within their grasp.

They lost not because they didn't want to win but because, over the course of the execution of their strategy, winning had slowly, almost invisibly lost its supreme importance. And thus at the moment when victory should have been theirs, they instead were accepting failure with a surprisingly calm and resigned sense of inevitability, accompanied by very eloquent and justified explanations about how it really wasn't their fault.

How does this happen?

Things usually start well—a project or the quarterly set of goals gets out of the gate and for a period of time is on track. Good numbers, honest and forthright accounts of how it is all going. Lots of back-patting and high-fiving. These are the "ops" reviews that are fun.

Then, as time goes on, challenges to progress arise; there are no clear answers or remedies, and the mischief begins. There is no obvious moment when the danger of failure comes riding in on a pale horse. But there is that moment—and everyone can feel it—when a project or the commitment to the promised results enters the risk zone.

It is precisely at this fork in the road—when egos and reputations get shaky—that leaders must recognize the signs of an impending crisis of confidence and intervene with specific messages and actions that can remedy the situation. This is one of those times when leaders earn their pay, in spades.

This breakdown can be described as the natural, human reaction to the cold-sweat realization that the hoped-for success is at risk and possibly in deep trouble. And the personal version of this is that someone is going to look bad, a career or two might be in jeopardy, and it is possible that heads will roll.

There are two basic operating modes for organizations under high-stakes execution pressure. One is the mentality of *winning*, which we know about; the other, less obvious to the untrained eye, is the disease of *failing elegantly*, a very sophisticated and veiled set of coping behaviors by individuals, the purpose of which is to avoid the oncoming train of embarrassment when the cover comes off the lousy results that we'd prefer no one ever sees.

This is the time when leaders must intervene with urgency and strength of conviction to get everyone on the high road—which we will call the *winner's mind-set*. This is the set of actions that offers the best chance of arresting the decline of faith, saving the game, and pulling out a victory. In the absence of this intervention, the momentum of *failing elegantly* will rule the day, and we'll be rewarded with a painful failure or shortfall, and a box full of stories and justifications absolving everyone on the field from any responsibility for this dismal outcome. The important elements of failing elegantly are (1) having a very sophisticated explanation for the loss, and (2) making sure we appear to have tried everything in our power to avoid this unwanted outcome. What this mentality forgets is the following harsh reality: *there are no style points for second place.*

Here's what *winning* and *failing elegantly* look like, as manifested in the three main behaviors that set up the chance to trip.

Tolerance

Tolerance is one of those "nice" concepts. We all want to be seen as tolerant people, and we try to teach tolerance to our children. But in an organization, in the effort to execute for success, it is a dangerous notion, mainly because without a clear line in the sand defining acceptable and unacceptable, a blurred line between success and failure follows. My experience tells me that under the pressure of performance expectations, there are two main camps of conversational commitment that describe the results to date from the field—and it is a leader's choice which one he or she tolerates:

> *Winner's Mind-Set*—What we want are insightful explanations for the gap between expected and actual performance—thoughtful cause-and-effect hypotheses. These are informed guesses—as informed and objective as they can be, untainted by the effort expended in dodging responsibility. There is tolerance of the simple fact that we don't have control over every variable in the game, so at times—through either forces outside our influence or simply not having run our best play—the results are not as we wish.
>
> *Failing Elegantly*—"The dog ate my homework" and other classic excuses arise—and they are tolerated. No results plus a good excuse is presented in lieu of results—and tolerated. Massive amounts of energy are poured into sophisticated justifications and rationalizations for certain courses of action, and there is veiled blame of everything outside the team's control. Everyone tolerates this transparent dissembling. Blame is a cancer. It is never "someone's" fault. There is no one in the phone book named "Someone."

Sloppiness

Leaders want to be good people, and they want show others that they have the wisdom to accept human frailty. So they allow themselves to tolerate a little sloppiness, a little imprecision, in their subordinates' work. But, please note, high-reliability organizations never allow sloppiness, because they know it equals *death*. By the same token, in your team, that same sloppiness ultimately means *failure*.

> *Winner's Mind-Set:* Zero tolerance. Sloppiness is 100-percent preventable. No mercy. Remind people they get paid to do high-quality, careful work. This is minimum acceptability. As soon as you cut a corner, you'll be tempted to cut another, and another—where does it stop?
>
> *Failing Elegantly:* The nice guy in you wants to avoid the perception of being a hardcore hard-ass and will politely look the other way, or catalog it away with some good-natured humor, allowing a corner to be cut, a report to be incomplete, or some shoddy work to pass as acceptable. Shoddy work and sloppiness almost always stem from being lazy or uncommitted or not having enough pride in the finished work.

Performance Feedback

One of the most pernicious points where failure can take hold is in the feedback process. Great leaders in execution crave the data coming back from the field, as it provides not only real-time measurement of their progress but also a reality check on their strategy. But these leaders, being eternally optimists and enthusiasts, also have a dangerous tendency to signal, often unconsciously, their dislike of bad news, their inner revulsion toward failure.

When that happens—especially when that leader hasn't regularly established an absolute demand for accurate, objective data—subordinates will begin to shape and color the data to meet that leader's hopeful expectations and emotional needs, rather than the leader's intellectual needs. When that happens, the feedback data starts becoming corrupted, and that in turn begins to undermine the overall strategy—until the likelihood of success itself begins to plummet.

> *Winner's Mind-Set*: Leaders demand that performance feedback data be delivered promptly and be uncolored, objective, plentiful, and robust. This data is used to figure out what is working and what isn't. Corrections to course and speed are made.

> *Failing Elegantly*: Subordinates begin to manipulate and editorialize the data, protecting themselves from blame or cause. They go to great lengths to explain why the numbers aren't really as bad as they look, or that the early returns don't paint the whole picture.

Leaders must demand high-road behavior here and keep the standards of excellence intact. It is extremely tempting to cut corners, move the goalposts, and accept impassioned rationalizations and justifications for substandard work and results. To give in feels like part of being a nice guy, being liked by your team, and understanding that "things happen." The problem is, succumbing to that temptation promotes a culture of mediocrity.

The mind-set of winners is paradoxically aligned with the maturity of their relationship with failure. You see, they don't think that the opposite of winning is *losing*. They see the other side of winning as *not winning yet*. And all the issues in between where they are now and the goal line are just clues and information they need to eventually achieve success. Just challenges that need to be tackled. They view the data associated with interim shortfalls and disappointments as *diagnostic* information that will help them correct course and improve their performance. They also resist the instinct to start doing real-time performance reviews—critiquing every member of the team who is part of the midcourse breakdown. They know the time for that activity comes later.

A tolerance for excuses, corrupt data that compromises strategy, and a distorted view of what is really happening "out there" is akin to boiling a frog one degree at a time—the frog can't tell how hot the water has gotten until it is dead. But if you put all these factors together and add the heightened sense of urgency that always characterizes the execution phase—an urgency that might become true hysteria as failures begin to mount—you'll have plenty of the necessary ingredients in place for systemic failure. The key factor is the resignation and rationalization that occurs when we conclude that winning seems out of reach.

Anyone who has ever been on such a dysfunctional team probably read that description with a shudder of recognition. These are dark moments. And you know what comes next: *When you stop believing you can win, you start devoting your energy to how best to lose.* Yet we all know that no one cares, or even remembers, who finishes in second place. We should leave it all on the field and, as the saying goes, "win or die trying." But when you've already begun to distance yourself from your absolute commitment to winning, you start blaming everything—your teammates, the strategy, bad luck, crooked competitors, insufficient support, and most of all, the man or woman in charge. In the case of the last, you are finally right.

The fact that many people—the honest and secure ones first— see what's happening and hold that behavior in contempt often proves to be an effective vaccine against the contagion spreading. And a certain amount of corrupted data is inevitable, not just because the sources want to fool you, but because they also fool themselves.

That said, the danger of not facing the truth head-on grows exponentially the more there is at stake, the greater the ultimate reward or punishment, and the greater the time and other pressures on the project. This world is a very competitive place, and even the simplest strategy takes focus and dedication to execute successfully. The eventual success of any major project or initiative, no matter how promising it may be at the outset, is never a foregone conclusion. So to add any *additional* handicap—shoddy work, corrupt data, a slacking off on the drive to ultimate victory—is simply unacceptable. The enemy should be outside the building, not in the mind-set of the team.

Once again, as has happened so many times in this book, we return to authenticity and trustworthiness. You have to be certain that the information you are being given is authentic and true. You have to be able to assume that everybody on your team can be trusted to put painful facts before comforting fictions. And you have to be able to look at the results of the team's efforts squarely and honestly—and not feel the need to wrap it in protective justifications, excuses, and blame.

Acceptance of failure is a cancer that can begin anywhere in the organization, then metastasize to every office, including your own. You can prevent it by setting clear and precise standards of behavior for everyone on the team, as well as clear consequences for the violation of those standards. And you can control it through continuous and open communication with every member of your team (some who will spot the problem before you do) and, where necessary, redundant processes and systems.

But most of all, you can cure the acceptance of failure by setting yourself as an example of zero tolerance of excuses (along with a welcome for honest admissions of error), of precision and care in all of your work, a clear-eyed focus on unvarnished results, and most of all, an unyielding and unwavering commitment to success.

That's what, as the leader, you've always owed your team. They need to be reminded that that's what they owe *you* in return.

The Essentials of Leading Execution

- Measure what matters to winning. Don't measure what is easy.

- Tackle the hard stuff early. Test the points of failure as quickly as possible. Don't avoid the tough questions early on—even if they can sink the plan.

- Persistence and flexibility are a balancing act—be committed, but stay open to feedback and be willing to change to succeed. You'd rather win than be right.

- Have a bias for action. Experiment. Learn. Seek feedback.

- Beware excuses and blame. There are two mind-sets: *winning*—or *failing elegantly*.

- The diagnostics of failure are priceless; you want the data that explains how you missed the goals. Cover-ups protect people from the embarrassment of failure, and they obstruct the necessary learning.

- Leaders must have a supreme, public, passionate commitment to winning and model it authentically in their personality and values.

PART THREE

CONSEQUENCE
Creating a Culture, Leaving a Legacy of Values

Whenever you do a thing, act as if the whole world is watching.

—Thomas Jefferson

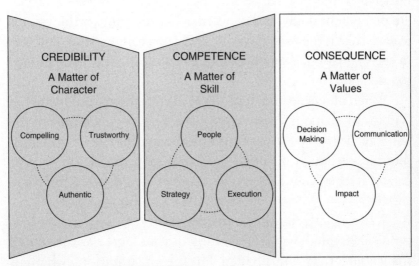

Figure P3.1. A Matter of Values

In the end, after your career is finished, what is left are the consequences of your leadership. It may seem counterintuitive, even vainglorious, to consider now a legacy that may not even begin for another decade or two, or more—and, indeed, may never be created at all if you fail at one of your first several leadership opportunities. But consider the alternative: most leaders begin to consider their legacy only in the twilight of their careers, when the die has pretty much been cast.

That's one reason why you see a flurry of activity among aging leaders to join nonprofit boards, establish foundations, sponsor university chairs, and so on. For some this is a natural next step in their lives, but for others it's a desperate rearguard action to fill in holes and paper over black marks on the final draft of the biography. A far better strategy is to *start* your career with an eye on your legacy, then maintain that focus through the years.

This is not so say that, in building a career legacy, you cannot make mistakes. As I've already noted, every great leader I know has not only failed, but failed spectacularly—and then used that failure almost as a talisman from that point on to guide them forward. The only failures that truly sink a career are the all-too-common breaches of integrity that destroy the faith of a followership and create permanent doubt and concern about the trustworthiness of a leader. Trust is the most fragile of assets; at a certain point, different in every situation, it simply cannot be restored to the level required to lead.

When all is said and done, legacy is not the official history; it is not your memoirs, nor even the words of your enemies; not the daily record of your executive decisions, nor your collected speeches—though all of those things may contribute to your legacy. Rather, your legacy is *the whole of what you leave behind as a leader*.

What exactly are the component parts of a legacy, and how is one assembled over time? Think of your legacy as the sum of the *culture* that you created for the organization, which is primarily about the larger community experience that affected everyone on the team, and your personal leadership *reputation*, which is almost entirely about the view that others have, individually, of you.

Legacy = Culture + Reputation

In Part Three of *Unusually Excellent*, we tackle the specific topics within culture and reputation that constitute our memory of the leaders we have known—(1) the way they communicated with us and our peers, (2) the way they made decisions that affected our quality of work and life, and (3) the way they treated us, as people, in the course of following their lead, and in the transfer of their influence to our own philosophy of leadership. I will address each of these in a separate chapter in this section.

Although you can choose the weight of your direct influence on culture building—a heavy hand or a light touch—the reality of both culture and reputation is that it will all come down to your behavior. Who you are and what you do will dwarf what you say, what you hope, or what you intend. It is all about what action you take—in the heat of battle, the pressure of producing the promised results, and the complexity of building teams and strategies. Your words *may* be important—but if, and only if, they match your actions.

Finally, in this track record of *doing*—not talking or hoping— it will be noted that your decisions, communications, and actions reveal, very clearly, your underlying *values*. Over time, there will be no confusion in the minds and hearts of those you lead as to what you stand for—what your *core values* truly are. So when you begin to reflect on the legacy that will be yours—and I hope you do that sooner rather than later—you will find it useful to start from your values, which brings us back to the very beginning of this book: authenticity. From there you can easily see how those values will shape your behavior over time. And from there, both culture within the organization and your personal reputation will follow. You can also see how so much of this is within your thoughtful control if you are willing to take the reins and chart your own course.

CHAPTER SEVEN

A LEADER'S COMMUNICATION
Open, Honest Dialogue

The biggest problem in communication is the
illusion that it has taken place.

—*George Bernard Shaw*

If you read a typical job description for a CEO or senior leader, written by a search firm or HR team after interviews with the other executives and board members, it will certainly contain a phrase something like this: "The candidate must be a *strong* and *skilled communicator.*"

Notice it does not say "a strong and skilled *talker*." It doesn't, because the very definition of a *communicator* is embedded in the fundamental expectations we have of leaders. Communication is *core* to leading—and it is a cornerstone of a leader's legacy. Most of the memories we have of leaders in our past include events or situations in which communication was a key part of the outcome and thus of our impression of that leader.

When we accept a role called *leader*, we implicitly agree to be the *chief communicator* for the organization. This accountability comes hand in hand with the authority of the job. It is not a responsibility to which we can opt in or opt out. Communication is to an organization like water to a garden—it keeps things vital, growing, and healthy. If plants or people are neglected, they show the signs of drought early and live in distress until we return them to a hydrated state.

The ability of leaders to communicate effectively is perhaps the highest leverage activity in their set of responsibilities. When they do it well, things work—smoothly and effectively. When it is done poorly, countless problems come out of the woodwork, all in response to the lack of good information available. Leaders must embrace this work and commit themselves to a high level of proficiency over the length of their careers as professionals. There is no substitute for effective communication—especially from the top of the organization. An enormous amount of resource goes to work every week in your organization trying to meet expectations. The least we should provide is the information and the connection that makes those efforts fruitful and satisfying. Communication is *essential* to leadership effectiveness.

If you think about it, you'll realize that much of what we experience as leadership actually occurs in a *conversation*. Conversations help ideas come to life and enable visions of the future to take shape and form. Conversations create meaning and context—they explain the things that confuse people. Perhaps most important, conversations make things happen—they help create direction and provide the inspiration for commitment and action. When something is not as you want it to be, chances are good that there is a conversation you need to have to fix it. I could beat this horse quite dead at this point, but the bottom line is that we expect and need our leaders to be superb communicators. This means we need them to craft the right messages, deliver them skillfully and effectively, and listen with engagement and empathy.

As followers, we have a basic set of questions that we expect will be answered—and reanswered, on a regular basis. Whether we voice it explicitly or not, this is a responsibility for which we hold our leaders accountable. And in the absence of the information that answers this set of questions, we get worried, distracted, or even paralyzed. We begin to concern ourselves with what we don't know and the missing data more than the work in front of us that awaits our attention. There is no question that we as leaders should not deny our teams the basic information that will allow them to keep their focus on their primary accountabilities.

The topics on your team's mind are predictable—the same ones exist in every organization, all the time, and it behooves you to design a process that keeps this information up to date for everyone on your team—at the intervals you decide appropriate.

The following are the topics we must speak to—and indeed answer—in our normal communications with our teams:

- What are we doing? (Vision and mission.)
- Why are we doing it? (Purpose and goals.)
- What's the plan to win? (What's the strategy here?)
- How are we doing? (Results and status—health of the business.)
- What is my part in the game? (What do you expect from me?)
- What's in it for me? (Why is this a compelling place for me to be?)
- How am I doing? (Give me feedback, acknowledgment, appreciation.)

Some of these items are best updated in a group setting; others are more appropriate one-on-one. But here's what I know for sure: if you commit yourself to keeping this set of questions answered on a regular basis, you'll avoid the downside of neglecting this obligation—which is that people will begin to speculate their own responses to all of these topics, conspiring with their peers, who also feel like they are in the dark. That is called a rumor mill, and nothing good ensues from it.

Keeping your talented team uninformed—on purpose, or by neglect—is just not a winning communications strategy in any way, shape, or form. Keeping them informed is one of your central responsibilities as a leader; it should be designed into your calendar and your leadership process. A shortage of accurate and timely information will predictably lead to anxiety, and over time anxiety will escalate to fear, unless you stop it in its tracks by helping your followers know what they must know so they can focus on their accountabilities and performance. Fear destroys the all-important sense of safety, and along with it go risk taking, innovation, and the quality of the information that flows within the organization.

Talking Trust

For leaders, the close relationship between trust and communication is often highlighted in large groups, where you have not only the challenge of authority and the hierarchy but also the public embarrassment factor—that career-limiting opportunity for somebody to ask you a really difficult question—and perhaps put themselves at risk by doing so.

Leaders always struggle in large group settings to get really difficult issues out on the table and to establish an environment of truly open and honest communications. And we've all seen what usually happens: the leader asks, "Are there any questions?" and is met by dead silence. This is exactly the opposite of what most leaders want.

One of the best solutions I've seen was devised by David Pottruck, former CEO of Charles Schwab. He appreciated that whenever there's power in the room there is also a great reluctance to ask questions. So, he decided, the only solution to get things flowing was to ask the tough questions himself.

And that's what he did. Standing in front of a large company meeting, he dramatically jumped off the stage and ran into the audience. There, he asked the empty stage the one question that they all wanted to ask but were afraid to: "Why aren't we getting bonuses this year?" Then he ran back up on stage and gave a thoughtful, honest, complete answer—proving that he was indeed willing to discuss the tough issues with everyone in the room—and in fact wanted to.

That broke the ice. Questions began to emerge—first the safe ones, and then some tougher ones, as the team warmed up and realized this was a safe place. Then, when one audience member asked a truly brave question, another one that everyone else was reluctant to ask, Pottruck thanked the employee and then asked the audience to give the man a standing ovation—thus stripping away much of their fear of speaking up.

It is Pottruck's experience and belief that the content of what he says as a leader is rarely remembered; what *is* remembered is how his words made listeners *feel*. In other words, although leaders usually focus on the information content of their communications, often what matters much more is the emotional content of that message and the connection—the leader's empathy with the audience. Did their time together make them feel more connected, or less? More trusting, or less? More energized, or less? If information were all that really mattered, leadership could be done by e-mail.

Of course, that doesn't mean that your communications can be content-free. Manoj Saxena, the former CEO of Webify (now part of IBM), has said that rumors are an organization's natural reaction to a lack of good data. I think he's right: people have an insatiable desire to know what they perceive as the truth—and if they don't get it, they'll invent their own version, and because it will be fear-based, it will certainly be worse than the official version you could share with them. Manoj even invented his own clever solution to the problem of rumors: in his all-hands meeting, he would hand out $100 bills to the three toughest and meanest questions from his audience—particularly the ones that raised a topic around which everyone knew there had been some buzz or speculation or anxiety—the stuff of rumors. What could have become a nasty situation instead became a lot of fun—and either defused the rumor mill or put it in its place. It gave him a way to connect—with authenticity and honesty—around issues that really matter. Over the long run, it created a demand for this forum, as everyone knew it was going to be useful, and safe, even fun at times.

Checklists and Guideposts

I hope the preceding narrative has convinced you of three key points: (1) communication is a core responsibility of leading—not an afterthought or side job; (2) most of the important things in organizations are the result of the right conversation having occurred; and (3) if you starve followers of their basic information requirements, you will pay a high price.

With those concepts established, let's move on to a larger advisory framework that can serve as a design guide and a checklist of the essential building blocks of conversations. This allows leaders to structure almost any communication against a robust checklist of things to think about and offers design points to ensure the purpose and goals of the intended conversation are met. This framework, not coincidentally, follows the basic rules of reporting and police detective work—a methodology designed to cover all of the characteristics of an event in the real world: what, when, where, why and how. This is a lot to cover, so I'm going to present it in the form of an expanded outline.

What—The "what" here is not content, per se. It is principle. Think through the *purpose* of your communication and ask yourself if there is a leadership topic underneath your specific message that needs an update or refresher—or one that will anchor your subject topic in a particularly powerful way. The principles of leadership we'll examine—the *five C's*—are topics that every leader should embrace and look for ways to reinforce and strengthen. These principles will guide your choice of words and topics and have enormous leverage in reminding the organization what matters.

A *Compelling Cause*—You need to give your subject a reason to participate, to join in your cause. That typically requires a vision, a mission, and a well-defined purpose. It's almost impossible for you to reinforce *cause*— especially the part that is personal to you—too often or too passionately.

Credibility and Competence—This is implicit in the reason you are even asking others to do a task: you believe that you have both the ability and the reputation to get them to listen and act. But there are times when a communication must have the additional purpose of reinforcing your competence or, through your authenticity and trustworthiness, your credibility. Don't take for granted that these things are always in perfect health.

Character—This is also implicit, and as we noted in the first part of this book, it is the reason other individuals are willing to stay and respect you enough to do a worthy job.

Commitment—You must make a commitment of your own before you can ask others to make theirs. And part of that commitment is that you will not abandon or betray them before the task is completed. Your commitment may be obvious to you, but it may not be to others—don't take that chance. Look for opportunities to remind the team of your personal stake in the matter.

Contribution—What impact will this action have? How does it matter? How does it add not just to your legacy but also to others'? What are their potential rewards for this action?

Why—We explore the underpinnings of the communication itself: *why* are you delivering this message at this time to this audience? Broadly speaking, intention falls into one of five categories, which I've made easier to remember by organizing them as *five E's*. Your communication may have, as its goal, one or two of these—or just as commonly, it will walk through each of them in turn. *What are you trying to create as the experience of your audience—be it one or many?*

Engagement—You want to get your target audience's attention. This may have the immediate goal of getting them to listen to what follows, or it may have the long-term goal of catalyzing or perpetuating an ongoing conversation between you and your followers.

Enrollment—Now that you've got their attention, you want to invite your followers to join you, to participate in your mission or the crusade. This process of enrollment, done properly, aligns the energy of your followers with your need for them to make a commitment to the cause. Don't underestimate simple questions like "Are you signed up for this plan, Fred?"

Energy—Energy itself must be stoked and fueled, because low energy inevitably leads to low action. Sometimes such a communication can act as a kick-off event— the spark that converts the strategy into execution.

Empowerment—As we've noted repeatedly, the job of the leader is not to execute but to lead followers in that execution. This can only be accomplished if you explicitly transfer ownership and accountability to your subordinates. It is crucial to make the transfer highly visible, both to remove any doubt and to empower those subordinates to make similar transfers to *their* subordinates.

Endorsement—The final purpose of leaders' communications typically occurs later in the execution of a task or at its completion. This is the apportioning of recognitions, awards, blessings, validations, and appreciations. As always, it is important to align these endorsements with the goals you set at the beginning of the project.

When—Timing is everything in communication. As a leader, you will receive some obvious and some not-so obvious clues from the organization as to when it needs communication in one form or another. Also, you should be looking for what's *missing* and filling that void with the appropriate communication. Anticipating the

needs of your team, or responding to demand for
information only you can supply, are key skills of the
leader-communicator.

Here are *six C's* to help you identify what's missing or to
synchronize the timing of your messaging.

   Context—A perspective on an action is almost never
      built into an action itself. You as leader have to
      provide that perspective, to enable others to fit it into
      the overall logic of the organizational strategy. Much
      of the time it is not obvious to our followers what
      something means—why it is important. Leaders help
      articulate meaning, and in doing so create under-
      standing and acceptance of what's so at any moment.
      This perspective is particularly useful when dealing
      with the consequences of *change* in all of its forms,
      including

   • Change itself: upsets, expectations, and discomforts

   • Conflict, including disagreements, arguments, and
      stand-offs

   • Choices, compromises, and consequences: trade-offs,
      risk/opportunity costs, and all of the factors that
      make up the "tyranny of choice"

   • Complexity and confusion: inevitable side-effects of
      change

   Confidence—There are times when the team needs a boost
      in confidence, a reminder of their capabilities and why
      you selected them. A well-timed, upbeat message or
      challenge can accomplish just that.

   Challenge—The right message, properly timed, can inspire
      your team to greater excellence. This can be done in a
      number of ways:

   • Goals: raising expectations, refining targets for a
      better fit, forcing the team to stretch to reach its
      real capabilities

- Standards: not just setting the high standards of performance that need to be met across the organization, but explaining the motives behind those standards

- Integrity: asking if we are behaving as we have promised we will and if we have fulfilled the social contract among ourselves and with our stakeholders

- Decisions: asking whether our decision-making process is optimal in terms of soliciting the best ideas, sorting through them objectively, and making the best possible final choice

Collaboration—One of the best times to deliver a message is when stresses and fractures begin to affect the cohesiveness of the team. Teamwork is an important competitive advantage, so you cannot allow it to be compromised. The best collaboration message is one that activates and reinforces communication among team members, which can often be accomplished by assigning tasks that demand this kind of communication. Going solo when teamwork is required is not an acceptable response to stress. You'd never see this happen in an HRO.

Culture—As a leader, you'll find there is no time more critical for effective communication than when the organization's culture is under threat, when the fundamental playing field of the team is at risk. But it can also be a positive moment—such as a new market thrust with a potentially large payoff. Whatever the cause, this is a moment when the sense of safety is most at risk among team members—and that fear must be answered by communication from you. The culture is the strongest fabric of support in the company; when all else fails, people lean on the culture to see how to behave, react, or feel. Take the time to reinforce the values you hold precious that define your culture.

Coaching—An excellent moment for the right message is when events conspire to create a teaching opportunity for members of your team. This can be based on either a success or a failure, and it is crucial that you pay considerable attention to the "who" of the situation, so that no one is either embarrassed or unjustifiably complimented.

How—Language and imagery are two ways we human beings communicate effectively with one another. It stands to reason, then, that any form of communication is improved through the skillful use of language, charts, and pictures. These are fundamentals that you learned in school but have likely allowed to slip just a bit—if so, it's time to sharpen up on the hows of communication. Let's review:

Clarity—Be organized, concise, and direct. Less is usually more. Get your message to a few, pithy essential points. Don't think simple can't be brilliant—the more concise the message, the more work it took to make it that way. Look at the Preamble to the Constitution and the Gettysburg Address: short and simple (in language, not content) is always superior to long and complex.

Consistency—Stay on message. Consult your previous communications to make sure that you are not contradicting what you said before—and if you must do so, incorporate an explanation as to why. Show the logical "bones" of your message.

Carefulness—Respect both the dignity and the intelligence of your audience, as well as the positional power of your own role. Do not abuse either. When in doubt, use qualifiers like "in my view" or "as far as I know."

Courage—Speak plainly, and eschew euphemisms, passive verbs, and "weasel words." Address tough issues plainly and honestly; speak directly to the fears of your audience. Put yourself in their shoes—they expect and deserve this from the leader of the organization. Where else should this come if not from the point of leadership?

Conviction—Think of the great speakers of history: not only did they have a powerful message and well-written text, but that text was written in such a way that it reflected their own personalities and speaking styles, which in turn enabled them to speak unforgettably from their deepest beliefs in what was possible. They used both the right words and their own convictions to create in the minds of their audiences a powerful and energizing vision of a better future.

Compassion—There is a dangerous, albeit natural tendency among leaders to make themselves appear larger than life, even infallible. But much worse is the concomitant tendency to wrap this attitude in a manner that suggests aloofness, coldness, and a lack of human feeling. Wise followers recognize this behavior as a sign not of superiority, but of fear, and as a source of concern, not respect. Great leaders are not afraid to show genuine emotion. They are empathetic to the problems of others—not just because it is the wise thing to do, but because, strategically, that one moment of humanity to a single "little" person can have more impact and resonance than a hundred speeches.

Completion—In most cases you are given only one chance to deliver your message. So deliver it—all of it. Close the deal; finish the message. Don't make the mistake of setting up the message, preparing the audience, delivering it brilliantly—and then neglecting to make the call to action. Notice how politicians, in their

television commercials and public debates, have
learned to ask for the viewer's vote? Communication
demands closure.

The Solitary Touch

The more people you lead, the less likely it is you will know who will
ultimately write your legacy. If you touch twenty thousand people
just once each, that one encounter—good, bad, or indifferent—will
define their memory of you forever. Even the tiniest, unconscious
message when voiced by a leader can be amplified like ripples on a
pond and create shocking repercussions. Here's just such a story.

Prior to his CEO tenure at Adaptec, John Adler was a senior
vice president at Amdahl, one of the pioneering computer companies of Silicon Valley. At Amdahl headquarters in Santa Clara,
John had a fairly long hallway that led to his office. One morning,
as he walked down that hallway, he encountered some maintenance guys who were doing some repairs. He greeted them with a
cheery, "Good morning" and, just to make some conversation,
noted that it must be difficult for them to work there because the
hallway was so dark. Then he went on his way, not giving the brief
encounter a second thought.

The next morning, when Adler came to work, he found five
maintenance men, all carefully replacing every light bulb in the
hallway. "What the hell are you guys doing?" he asked, surprised to
see such a flurry of activity for no apparent reason.

"We're replacing the light bulbs, boss," was the reply. "You said
it was too dark in here."

At that moment, John realized that, like it or not, every word
he said on the job carried an added—even an absurd—weight.
Even the words that had been misinterpreted.

No doubt those workers, on hearing Adler's remark the first
morning, had concluded that he was giving them a message,
perhaps even making a polite request by his comment. Or perhaps
they had just thought: hey, if we change the light bulbs the boss will

notice us again—and maybe compliment us—and that'll help our jobs. They probably even had a meeting about it, and when other maintenance people heard about it, they demanded to be allowed in on the Great Light Bulb Changing. Perhaps there were even a few fights over who deserved the opportunity to be part of this big moment—all because of a simple, off-the-cuff remark by a leader who promptly forgot the encounter.

Every conversation with, and every communication from, a leader carries added weight because of the authority of the position behind it. Have a bad day and snap at one of your subordinates, and that person may go back to a cramped cubicle and start updating the résumé, or go out and get drunk, or miss a night's sleep. Your momentarily bad day could be their nightmare—and something they will remember forever. Your mood matters; don't make it their problem.

And never forget: when the differential of title and power is sufficiently great, there is really no such thing as a "casual" conversation.

Moreover, this "open mic" has no boundaries: remarks you make on the golf course, at the supermarket, in the hotel bar, and words you write in memos, emails, text messages, and tweets—especially the wrong ones—can carry far greater weight than that carefully composed and edited letter to shareholders under your photo in the annual report, or that precisely orchestrated interview with the reporter from the local TV station.

Yet, as with broadcast professionals and public figures, the presence of this perpetual threat can't be allowed to interfere with the conduct of one's career. In fact, I'm going to argue in this chapter that despite this continuous risk, as a leader you need to communicate with your followers even *more* than might be your natural inclination.

Your 24 × 7 Job

We tend to think of leaders as being men and women of action. But in fact, if you look over the entire length of a career, great leaders can be more accurately characterized as men and women of communication. Indeed, before and after everything, the leader is the *chief communicator* of the organization. As such, the leader has three basic tasks:

- Align the interests, energy, and commitment of the team.
- Reduce fear, confusion, and anxiety.
- Instill confidence and trust, while rallying support and contributions.

I challenge every leader reading this to sit down at the beginning of every week, and ask him- or herself whether there are any conversations that need to happen in those next five days that they should initiate or request, that would achieve one or more of these objectives. Clearly I consider leadership communication to be a core, critical process—not an afterthought, filler, or annoyance. In fact, I consider communication to be so important that all leaders should consider themselves to *be the message*—that is, to live out their careers in congruence with the beliefs, morals, and truths embedded in their communication. That means that every time you speak or send a message to your team, you need to ask yourself: *What values are being revealed and modeled in this message, and are they congruent with the values I hold and that I want this organization to hold?*

It is important to remember every day that communication goes both ways, and that Unusually Excellent leaders in my experience almost always listen much more than they speak. And they don't just listen as a managerial duty, or out of politeness: rather, they *listen with a purpose*.

What does that mean? It means listening intently, without interrupting, judging, or fixing blame. It means listening past the message to the speaker's interests, talents, and values. It also means listening for what *you* value: commitment, a willingness to join in, a sense of teamwork. Finally, it means listening for opportunities: to move things forward, to provide what's missing, to develop a relationship. So much of what we leaders crave, and need, to be successful with our teams is right there for the asking—if we stop to listen.

It is not through edicts, but through this two-way communication between leader and followers, through authentic dialogue targeted toward achieving common goals, that leader-follower communication becomes a form of storytelling—a personal exchange, founded on mutual trust, using a common language with terms that are uniquely resonant for the participants, with both an immediate and a larger purpose.

This kind of storytelling is the precursor to the creation of a true organizational *culture*—the body of practices, stories, mores, myths, and legends, proprietary language, and modes of social interaction that is unique to the enterprise, that defines it, and that distinguishes it from all other enterprises. A great organizational culture can last for generations and serve the enterprise over the long term as its single greatest competitive factor.

It is also likely to be your most important and enduring legacy.

The Essentials of Leadership Communication

- The most senior leader is the default chief communicator.

- Honest information is the pure water of the organization.

- Leadership is a conversation. Commit yourself to learning how to have all kinds of conversations. This a skill, and you can become incredibly proficient through practice and feedback. Don't restrict yourself to the conversations that are comfortable for you.

- This chapter isn't titled "Talking." Communication is a connection. Listening is often the best way to communicate. Listen like there is only one engine of four still working on the airplane and the pilot just came on the public address speakers to give you instructions for the crash landing.

- Expectations are established through communication.

- Feedback is worth its weight in gold. Praise is like fertilizer for others' self-esteem. Catch someone doing something good, and let him or her know why you appreciate his or her behavior or work. When praise is warranted, don't skimp or ration it.

- The following questions are always looking for an answer: *What are we doing? Why? How will we win? What do you expect of me? How am I doing?*

CHAPTER EIGHT

A LEADER'S DECISION MAKING
Values-Based Choices

> It's not hard to make decisions when you know
> what your values are.
>
> —*Roy Disney*

The final judgment of our leadership expertise will depend, more than anything else, on the quality of the decisions we have made, in aggregate, over the course of our careers as leaders. Leading decision making is, in essence, leading the conversation that improves the quality of those decisions. Your primary job as a leader is not to make most of the decisions that arise every day, but to lead in such a way that the people who *do* make them make better decisions than they would alone.

That much should be obvious to the reader. After all, if strategy is the adaptation of planning to the real world competition and conflict, then decision making is the real-time response of leadership to the twists and turns and unexpected challenges of execution. Sure, leaders also make decisions during the planning process, and sometimes those decisions can be decisive, but it is the series of decisions made under pressure, in the heat of battle, that makes careers and sets legacies.

When you look at the lives of great leaders you admire, aren't those game-time decisions the ones you most admire and remember—and isn't that the very definition of legacy?

If we examine decision making—both the art and the science—there is a structure to consider and a number of powerful and useful principles to keep in mind.

Decisions are responses to both problems and opportunities. Thus they are both challenges that come at us (to which we react) and choices we make proactively (to seize the opportunity or direct the action). Either way, we are presented with some alternatives, and in the choice that ensues we lay down another plank of our leadership reputation.

In a perfect world, decision making would be simple—just respond to the issues as the action unfolds in front of you, or get the right people together and make a decision. But, as we all know, in the real world there are endless ways for this process to break, sometimes catastrophically.

For example, internal communications channels can falter, and a problem will fail to rise to a level where there is someone empowered to tackle it. As a result, the problem just sits there, unresolved, an open wound that can continue to grow until someone in authority recognizes it—and sometimes it is too late. Or the problem can rise to a level in the organization far above where it should have been addressed, forcing senior executives—even the top leader—to waste their valuable time in trifles while other, more pressing problems await action. Sometimes the problem temporarily stops at a person who has neither the authority nor the power to make the call. And sometimes, out of fear of punishment from above, team members will ignore a problem or mischaracterize it or hide it in hopes that it will eventually go away—which it rarely does.

So how do you improve your chances of consistently making the smartest decisions even under maximum duress?

Decision Structure

The structure of leading decision making appears simple on the surface but, as with many things, the devil is in the details. The following are the categories and the *sequence* of thinking to consider as you approach this extremely important competency:

What? What exactly are we deciding?

When? When should, or must, this decision be made?

Who? Who decides?

How? How will the decision be made?

It is obvious that "what" is the starting point—we need to know what, precisely, we are deciding. However, you may wonder why I positioned "when" ahead of "who" or "how." Quite simply, the perceived urgency of a decision often determines both the choice of who makes it and, accordingly, how it is made. And we usually know the "when" as one of the first aspects of the decision at hand. If something is truly urgent, and there is someone nearby and available who is appropriately qualified to make the decision, it probably makes sense to let that person decide, even if he or she is the not absolute best person if the urgency was not high. If there were more time, it might be possible to route that decision to someone even more qualified to decide.

The urgency of a decision can certainly be dramatized or overblown, and there are certainly more false alarms than legitimate emergencies. Nonetheless, knowing the true time frame in which something should or must be decided will certainly shape the choice of who decides and how the decision gets made.

What Exactly Are We Deciding?

As silly as it sounds, the topic of a decision, as originally formulated and communicated, can drift and morph over the course of a long debate or heated discussion. I've been in dozens of conversations where an issue was being debated and, after some vigorous conversation, it was suddenly obvious that the decision we thought we were making was not necessarily the decision originally raised.

It helps to write down, or to speak in painfully clear terms, exactly what the decision is on the table. Ask the person raising the issue: "What precisely is the decision you wish to discuss?" To further refine a topic with some rough edges, you can ask: "What are some of the possible answers or decisions that you could imagine us considering?" When you hear the form of some of the possible answers, you'll better understand the legitimate core of the decision at hand.

I was recently reminded, firsthand, of one of the most telling distinctions concerning "What are we deciding?" through a conversation with a client.

On arriving at the office of Mike, the client CEO, I started with the normal: "What do you think we should talk about today?" Mike had a pressing topic ready for our meeting: the recent performance of his vice president of marketing. As I dug in and asked a few more questions, I realized that although he had framed it as an *if* question, it really wasn't one; it was a *how* question. I had seen this confusion before—*there is a huge difference between something you've already decided and something you haven't*. And if you have already decided, you are likely asking about *how*, not *if*. The actual conversation went like this:

MIKE: John, I wanted to talk about some performance issues with my VP of Marketing, Robert.

JOHN: OK, tell me more.

MIKE: Well, he has missed some significant commitments over a long period of time, and I'm not sure he is going to scale to the demands of the job as I see it going forward. I'm concerned. What should I do?

What unfolded from there, through my inquiry, was a situation in which Mike had indeed already decided that Robert was not going to make it, and he wanted to make a change.

JOHN: It sounds like you have already decided something here, and in fact, you are really asking me about *how* to proceed from here, not *if* you should do it. Right?

MIKE: Yes, I guess that's right. I think I have decided, and I guess
I just didn't realize it until I had said it to you. I thought I was
still debating it in my mind, but the truth is, I've decided, so
we should talk about *how*. Although I would like to know if
you agree with the direction I'm headed in.

In this moment, I realized how common it is to think we are in
the *if* stages of a decision when we are really in *how*. We have already
decided something, but we haven't told anyone—including,
sometimes, ourselves. This is a useful difference to notice, as you
then know how to revisit *if*, should that be appropriate. Or perhaps
the correct next step is to confirm or affirm that the decision has
actually been made, and move to the one not yet made.

What Flavor Is This Decision?

Staying with the *what* of the decision-making structure, it is clear
we often tend to think of decisions as being monolithic, a collection of facts, figures, and speculations that we must drill through to
come up with a thoughtful and rational decision. But we all know
that in real life this is rarely so. Instead, decisions are usually defined
by three distinct characteristics, each challenging a different part of
our character.

Empirical

Decisions can be classified as either *simple* or *complex*. The degree
of complexity is usually determined by *data*: how much information is needed to make an intelligent decision and how much of
that data is actually available. How leaders interpret these factors
usually depends on their personality. Some leaders are prepared
to make decisions based on limited or even faulty information.
They are typically described as "decisive," when in fact they may
merely be impetuous. Others wait until they have every bit of
information before they finally make their decision—and risk

missing the window of opportunity for success. They are described as everything from "patient" and "prudent" to "indecisive" and "cowardly."

There is a right moment to decide, when the data is sufficiently complete and clear relative to the cost and time required to mine the long tail of additional information—and that moment is called the "knee of the curve." It varies with each situation, and it's important that you, as a leader, know that the perfect moment—between impatience or reaction and having the whole of the data set in hand—does exist, and that the people you enlist to help you will know it too. But when they seem stuck or stymied, yearning for more data so they can increase their odds of being right, it is your job to intervene and make the call.

A subset of this set of decision types occurs when the data is so confusing or so unclear that it serves no purpose in the decision except to paralyze the process. In these cases, the spectrum of simple to complex loses its value, and the decision needs to shift to another criteria—like intuition. When the data is that confusing or unclear, you have to trust your gut—or, if possible, postpone the decision until you can get better data. It is hard to look smart with bad data.

Principle

Decisions can also be characterized as *easy* or *difficult*. Easy decisions typically have either one obvious solution or few real consequences, or both. Again, human nature is such that these easy decisions are almost always snatched up way down in the organization—it's a cheap way to score points with superiors and look like you're in command. Meanwhile, the tough ones are kicked upward until they reach someone who is either brave enough to take it on or, more likely, has no choice. The buck has stopped on their desk.

This cherry-picking of easy decisions, made for political rather than pragmatic reasons, is yet another reason why Unusually Excellent leaders enforce institutional cultures that drive decision making back down the org chart, placing responsibility on the people best positioned and equipped to make the decision, not merely awarding it by default to the person who can get the most advantage out of it.

In the very best organizations, leaders create a culture based on the *principle* of personal autonomy and responsibility, in which decision making is not only pushed down to the right people, but those acts are subsequently recognized and rewarded by the rest of the team—while buck-passers are shunned as grandstanders. This culture is very difficult to develop, mainly because it goes against most people's natural risk aversion, but ultimately it creates value in both the speed of decision making and the quality of the decisions.

Emotional

Finally, there are *pleasant* and *unpleasant decisions*. You know what to do, but it just isn't going to be much fun. Needless to say, everybody likes to make pleasant positive decisions—honoring the hard work of subordinates, doling out promotions, choosing the better of two good opportunities, and so on. There are even pleasant (at least to some people) negative decisions, such as firing someone who more than deserves it, or getting out of a business that has proven to be nothing but trouble.

But nobody likes to make or communicate unpleasant decisions such as disappointing subordinate's expectations of their true performance level, taking away a responsibility that was valued by someone but that should not be theirs at this point, or delivering tough-to-hear performance feedback—including letting people go from the organization in a humane but clear fashion. Public admissions of failure, mass layoffs, retreats from the field, announcements of poor results—these are all classic examples of necessary, but unpleasant decisions and the communications that follow. They are similar in that they all combine a wounding to one's ego along with the heartbreaking knowledge of the injury one's own poor leadership has done to others. At such moments you wonder why you ever wanted to be a leader in the first place, whether you will ever wish for such authority again—and you understand why some famous historical leaders have chosen to fall on their swords.

When Does This Decision Need to Be Made?

The speed of decision making is essentially the cycle time of the organization. Nothing determines an organization's ability to move in its market with agility and speed so much as its ability to make decisions quickly and efficiently. I need not remind you we live and work in a fast-paced world. The best proxy for the "clock speed" of an organization is the efficiency with which decisions are made and the subsequent actions are implemented. Time is the great equalizer, and we all have exactly the same amount to use each day. Time also waits for no one, and you can never retrieve a lost hour, day, month, or quarter. It is often shocking to look up and notice that a week or two has evaporated and a decision you thought would have been made by now is still stuck somewhere.

We know that time is a double-edged sword—it can be our friend if the data is changing and we are managing risk. We'd like to know more if we can, especially if there is no consequence to delaying things for a while. And it can be our enemy in a "time to market" or similar situation in which the swift are rewarded for expedience. So it is important to know on which side time is located—with you or against you.

To help make that determination, leaders should ask these questions:

- When do we have to make this decision? Why?
- What is the cost of waiting?
- How fast will we get feedback to know whether we have made a good decision?
- What ability do we have to correct a mistake if we are wrong?

- What is the advantage or necessity to make the decision now?

Don't ever let someone keep you from thinking things through before you decide. Failure to give a decision the necessary thought leads to a high probability of buyer's remorse, because it moves the decision from logic to emotion, which is a less reliable process (except when it involves matters of the heart). You usually have more time than you think.

Ultimately, the all-important speed of operations you want to inculcate in your team depends as much on you as on them, because total operational speed is a three-variable equation:

$$\text{Total Cycle Time} = \text{Time to Decide} + \text{Time to Commit} + \text{Time to Execute}$$

Note that the first two variables depend mostly on your leadership; only the last process is driven by your team. Yet leaders typically put most of the pressure on the last process—time to execute—when the real delays that determine the success and failure of the operation are just as likely to occur in the decision or commitment phase.

This is a perfect example of the adage "Your lack of planning is not my emergency." I'll wager every reader of this book has experienced at least once in their career a situation in which they were blamed for not accomplishing a task that simply could not be completed in the time given—and wondered what happened in the interval between when the problem was recognized and when it was finally given to them to solve. Nothing so effectively destroys morale—and pushes staff to update their résumés—as being left holding the bag for other people's indecisiveness.

As often as paralysis occurs in the "time to decide" phase, it happens even more often when it is time to commit. This is basic human nature. You can convince yourself that you are moving things forward, gathering support from team members, and being decisive—all while leaving in your back pocket the option, even after you've announced your choice, of *not actually doing it*.

In the nomenclature we've used in this book, it is easy to be dynamic and decisive during the planning stage, but when a leader reaches that jumping-off point where preparation becomes execution and planning becomes strategy, suddenly, in the face of real, measurable consequences that will impact the leader's reputation and legacy, he or she may come up short on courage.

Who Should Make This Decision?

Unless you create a corporate culture that rewards (or punishes) otherwise, the natural human tendency is to shirk making a decision about anything that can be pushed up the organization chart to someone else. This in turn eventually results in a team environment in which all of the easy problems are dealt with lower in the organization, while all of the tough ones end up at the top.

Although this arrangement may seem flattering to you as leader—after all, it proves how irreplaceable you really are—it is ultimately self-destructive. For one thing, it reinforces contempt at both ends of the scale: senior management begins to treat the rank-and-file as lazy and incompetent, while lower-level team members start kicking everything difficult upstairs, then sit back in judgment of the successes and failures of their leaders.

The proper answer to the question *Who decides who decides?* is that the person who is best equipped—by skill, experience, proximity, and past relationship—to make the decision in that particular case should be the person to assume that duty. Therefore you as leader need to create—and constantly reinforce—an institutional culture that drives decision making down the organization chart and out to the individual who is best equipped to make the decision.

How do you do this? There are several proven ways:

1. *Push back*—As flattering as it is to be seen as the final arbiter of all things, you need to hand off high-impact, high-visibility

decisions to subordinates who are better equipped than you are to deal with that particular problem.

2. *Reinforce*—Inform your lieutenants that you expect them to follow your lead in delegating both responsibility and authority—and base part of their performance evaluation on their willingness to do so.

3. *Reward*—Single out low-level team members and publically recognize and reward them for exhibiting independence and initiative.

Is there a risk to this type of leadership? Sure there is. There's always the underqualified and overambitious team member who tackles a problem that is beyond the member's ability. And just as it is natural for people to kick problems upstairs, so too is there an understandable tendency for senior leaders to not want to surrender even a tiny part of their fate to less-experienced subordinates.

But I would submit—and the stories of great organizations from IBM to Hewlett-Packard to the U.S. Army in Normandy to NASA during the Apollo program underscores my argument—that you are *always* better off in the long run driving decision making down to the right people than in letting it drift upward in the organization. Sure, there will be mistakes, but whatever is lost in experience is usually more than made up in the speed of response, the time devoted to studying the problem, and the customization of the solution. Finally, as we discussed in the last chapter, strong two-way communication up and down the organization will not only help spot people taking on more than they can handle but also mobilize help if needed.

When we know everything we reasonably can about the decision, including the real time frame in which it must be made, then we can decide who should make the decision at hand. Normally, we'd say, as in the HRO discussion of Chapter Six, that a decision should be made at the lowest level possible in the organization—and no lower. Ideally, the person closest to the situation and most knowledgeable of the specific circumstances should decide anything appropriate to the level of risk and consequence inherent in the choice.

However, what we often find is a pattern whereby the same people—and perhaps the wrong people—just keep making a decision or a set of decisions because "that's the way we've always done it." Another sloppy behavior is to just push decisions up the chain that could be made at lower levels—a practice known as "upward delegation."

It is a good practice for senior leaders and teams to review the decisions they are making and ask themselves what would have to be installed in the organizational machinery to push decision making to the levels appropriate for each decision. That would allow decisions to be made faster and likely with better data—a double benefit of getting the decision made where it belongs, instead of where it drifts.

Don't Wait; Decide

Notwithstanding our efforts to route decisions to the right person or level in the organization and avoid gratuitous upward delegation, one thing is undeniably true—*decisions demand to be made*. Unmade decisions stop the action—even worse, they can stop that action in ways that are inexplicable even to team members. No one knows why nothing is progressing. They assume that something has gone wrong: a bad judgment, an unexpected shift in the environment, a major screw-up somewhere. But in fact, the real problem is that the action has stalled because a crucial decision was never made. So while everyone is running around looking for solutions or someone to blame, the real problem lies elsewhere, in decision paralysis.

In the hierarchy of decision failure, not making a decision is almost always worse than making a bad decision. Bad decisions, as long as they aren't utterly ill-advised and catastrophic, at least keep the organization moving in pace with changing events—and thus can often be rectified by a course correction.

Not making a decision at all, although it may seem the safe choice—because, intellectually, it positions you to make the right move when the reality of the situation is more revealed—actually strips your organization of its momentum, stalling it at the starting line, and makes it highly unlikely that you can ever get up to speed in time to be a serious player.

Chasing Decisions

Unusually Excellent leaders don't just make decisions, they pursue them. Because the speed of the organization is often its destiny— and because that speed directly correlates with the speed with which its decisions are made or not made—these leaders are haunted by the fear that somewhere in the organization a critical decision is being left orphaned and unmade.

This fear turns these Unusually Excellent leaders into detectives. They use the two-way information apparatus they've emplaced to search the organization for these unmade decisions and expose them to the light of day. They reinforce the institutional culture they've created to honor team members who take on the tough decisions—and when that fails, they at least keep the decision moving up the organization chart until it reaches someone who *will* respond.

Finally, as a last resort, these leaders are prepared to intervene at any time and at any moment to break a gridlock—assigning the decision to someone who can make the decision, or making it themselves. Obviously, this intervention must be done judiciously, recognizing that others may be humiliated and/or angry, but also with the understanding that much is at stake and time is of the essence.

Some decisions, and the communication of them to follow, simply must be made by the top leader in the path of that issue. We can wish or hope or dream that someone else will deal with a difficult issue, but at some point, when it isn't happening below us, the better strategy is to just grab it back and make it. There is no value in denying that some issues just drift up the organization, and it is far better to end the delay by making the decision than to hope against hope that someone else will. This is one of the things leaders get paid for.

There is, of course, a danger in this behavior—and if you are like me, you've probably been a victim of it. It is the leader who—for reasons of ego, fear, or impatience—starts making a habit of these interventions. The inevitable result is damaged morale, widespread resentment, and that decline in productivity that we've already shown results from a climate of fear. When you never know if the boss is going to swoop in at a critical moment and publicly take responsibility away from you, two things happen:

1. You try to never again be forced into a position where you have to make a decision—usually by foisting those decisions off on others.

2. When you *must* make a decision, you hide the fact you are doing so (often by not getting the advice and assistance you need) until it is too late for anyone to intervene.

It is not hard to imagine the damage this can do to an organization's health. So you should always be armed with this knowledge of the potential consequences when you make your decision to intervene in your subordinates' decisions. This doesn't mean you should never do so, but you had better make damn sure there is no alternative. And you had better be prepared to deal with the fallout afterward.

Finally, keep in mind that a decision not communicated is often the equivalent of a decision unmade. If a tree falls in a forest and no one is around to hear it, does it make a sound? If a decision is made and no one finds out, is it a decision? Decisions made mean a choice about what to do next. That decision must be communicated to the people who are affected, need to know, or must take some action. The communication of decisions is the final opportunity to botch it—or to nail it.

There are myriad ways to decide something. I can't advise leaders, through a book, how to pick the right approach; the specifics of the circumstances at hand will determine that. But I *can* say that it is useful to explicitly state how a decision will be made, especially if that methodology is sensitive or important to the team, which it often is.

Where does legacy fit in with all of this? It provides *perspective*. Rarely does a single decision determine how the world will remember you. And even when it does, that decision often arrives disguised as a matter of lesser importance. (Remember, "For want of a nail . . . a kingdom was lost.") When you make decisions in the heat and emotion of the moment, it is easy to make foolish mistakes—unless your decision-making process includes a recognition of how each of these decisions fits into the larger context of your entire career and all of the decisions you will make in that career. Again, this larger perspective shouldn't paralyze you into making *no* decision—after all, as we've just seen, when it comes to one's legacy, lack of decisiveness is one of the worst errors of all.

The key is to make your decisions at the moment when timing and the best available information for your decision converge, and to make that decision promptly and with your full commitment to support its best possible execution. And you need to *own* that decision—and to have the discernment to recognize that if it is not yours to own, you should put it in the hands of the right person in the organization for the job, wherever that person may be, and then support and trust them to do the job.

Finally, as leader, you need to recognize that ultimately not only will many of the most difficult decisions finally end up in your lap, but the most unpleasant ones will land there too. When faced with these high consequence decisions, you need to stay on top of your emotions, good or bad, and not allow them to unduly impact your decisions. Over the course of your career, every decision you make should reflect your deepest values—not merely expediency, your mood at the time, or short-term advantage.

Unusually Excellent leaders recognize that the organizations they run are only as good as the decisions they make—so they create and cultivate an institutional culture that both rewards smart, fast decision making and inculcates a sense of personal responsibility when it comes to those decisions. In the final analysis:

$$\text{Quality of decision} = \text{Quality of human process} + \text{Quality of information}$$

As a leader, you should strive for the best people you have to be aligned with the most important decisions, and build the information infrastructure that supports the speed and detail that crucial decisions deserve.

Remember: the future will be watching.

The Essentials of Decision Making

- Most decisions model a value somewhere in them—*why* and *how* we do things. The memory of the value that was revealed or reinforced will outlast the memory of the decision.

- Decision speed is a proxy for and predictor of organizational cycle time.

- You should be deciding only difficult things—nothing that anyone else could decide. With difficult decisions, it's often a choice between bad and worse.

- Difficult versus unpleasant decisions: Decisions are difficult when the data is just not clear, the consequences are high, and it is hard to change the call. Unpleasant decisions are not difficult to make in your mind and heart—they are just uncomfortable to communicate.

- Deciding who decides is key. Unmade decisions have no owners.

- Hunt down and expose unmade decisions with relentless energy. They stop the action, and they hide everywhere in the organization. They are sand in the gears of progress.

- Decisions made should align with and add power to spoken priorities.

- There are some decisions that you must make—the buck really does stop at your desk.

CHAPTER NINE

A LEADER'S IMPACT
The Transfer of Influence from Leader to Follower

The supreme quality for leadership is
unquestionably integrity. Without it, no real success
is possible, no matter whether it is on a section
gang, a football field, in an army, or in an office.
—*Dwight Eisenhower*

Of all of the issues of leadership and legacy, none is more complex, elusive, and unpredictable than your work with people—the relationships, transactions, conversations, interactions, conflicts, shared victories, and all the rest. These are the memories that have the most juice for most leaders and most followers. That's why I've saved this conversation for last.

There is also a reason why Parts One and Three "bookend" the nuts-and-bolts part of leadership covered in Part Two—the game-day activity of leading people, developing strategy, and executing action. Part One was all about preparing to lead with influence and impact. Just as important, the first third of this book explained why it is that before you can lead you must earn the *right* to lead—and that comes down to credibility.

Part Three, which we are now completing, is the flip side of preparing to lead. Here we have been looking at the *impact* of leadership—the summing up that normally happens only at the end of a career—when, frankly, it is too late to do much about it.

I'm suggesting as the *central idea* in this chapter: *even though you can't fully know the ultimate impact of your leadership, you can learn to imagine or even predict that your legacy will be based on how you are leading today.* You can become much more aware of those moments that might preview how your leadership track record will be regarded over time. And that might be enough to influence your actions in dealing with subordinates long before you decide to hang up your spikes.

What I'm *not* endorsing here is an obsession with your future reputation so fervent as to inspire you to micromanage everything you do now as if you could know exactly how it will all be assessed years down the road. That would simply not serve you as a leader in any way. In golf, we call this "steering the ball" instead of just swinging naturally and letting the ball go where it will. Golfers make their best swings when they just focus on the process and detach from the results. Your influence as a leader is a function of leading authentically, present to the moment, doing your very best with the challenges in front of you, paying no particular attention to your imagined assessment of your behaviors at some point in the future.

There is, however, a great advantage available, should you choose to lead today with an appreciation of how your actions, decisions, and communications will be viewed in time by the very people currently under your command. This point of view will serve to broaden your perspective and bolster your courage to do the right things in the face of pressure and temptations. It will bring you back home to fundamentals and first principles—those things you intuitively know will be remembered and valued by others down the road.

Leader Taking the High Ground

This one is about leadership courage, accountability, integrity, and credibility.

In 1999, SystemTech was coming off a very good year in 1998, but also knowing that it faced a tough year ahead—mostly because the Y2K fear was dominating the entire digital world, and SystemTech didn't sell any Y2K products.

But the company also knew that it was about to face the consequences of a previous strategic blunder: over the preceding eighteen months it had failed to make the crucial transition from an enterprise client-server platform to a web-based service. And it was now painfully obvious that they were at least a year behind their competitors.

Somehow, though, SystemTech managed over the course of the next few months to dodge the biggest of these bullets. CEO Jeff Smith stood before the board at the end of the year and, with characteristic truthfulness, declared the year a mild tactical success but a strategic failure. They had somehow scraped in enough business to salvage the year financially, but they were suffering from their failure to have their plans for the Web in place for their key customers—and that oversight was apparent in the anemic forecast for Year 2000.

Other, lesser leaders might have wiped the sweat off their fore-heads, said a small prayer for their survival, and gone back to the same business. But Smith was dedicated to making sure this kind of near-disaster never happened again.

So he proposed to the board that the executives who had developed the company's plan—which included the whiff on the Web—be given just 50 percent to 75 percent of their bonuses, in spite of achieving 95 percent of their operating plan for the year. What's more, Smith recommended that he get just 30 percent of the bonus due to him.

Why those numbers? Because, as Smith explained it, he should be penalized for the strategic failure—and should receive only a portion of the reward for the moderately successful operating results, because that was largely his team's job. And although the team should get most of their bonus for the current year results, they were all at fault for the plan they developed together—which included a massive strategic oversight and one that was clearly preventable.

In other words, Smith thought: *If you guys play the wrong music, it's my fault. If you play it badly, it's your fault. I can't play the horns or the violin for you, but I can put the wrong music in front of you, and I can direct you poorly—and that's exactly what I did.* The larger message of Smith's remarkably precise decision is that although the leader is the most responsible person on the team, that responsibility is also shared, to some degree, by everyone else on the team.

The executive team was furious. They felt like this violated the tacit agreement that *If I shovel eight pounds of dirt for a dollar, then you give me the dollar.* But Smith reminded them that they had all made the commitment to be all-in with both the successes and the failures of the company. His first message—and an Unusually Excellent leader like Jeff Smith always turns crises into a teaching moment—was that when we commit, we commit all the way. And when we have a failed strategy, we are all responsible—and me most of all.

Smith's second lesson to his team was that everyone in an organization has a boss—even the leader. In Smith's case, this was the board of directors. Thus he was accountable, just as they were accountable—and as they all shared in the rewards of success, so too did they all have to accept the penalties of failure.

In the end, Smith didn't lose a single member of his team.

Whisper Campaign

The first thing we must understand is the nature of our impact as leaders and the factors that compose a leader's career legacy. This legacy is not monolithic, but is composed of *three* parts, each dealt with in a different manner.

The two most obvious ways that leaders have an impact, and ultimately create a legacy, are through our *decisions* and our *successes*.

Looking back over the course of their careers, the greatest regrets of most leaders typically stem from either poor decisions they made, or results that didn't match their (or the world's) expectations. Life doesn't give us many mulligans, so most of the decisions we make and the victories and defeats we experience are facts of our past that we must live with forever. At best, we can hope and pray that, somehow, the perceived failures or mistakes will age well over time—and that history will render a better judgment on us than we currently give ourselves. We aren't alone: note how all the recent U.S. presidents—Bush father and son on the two Iraq wars, Clinton on international terrorism, and Obama on economic bailouts—currently await the redemption of history to whitewash the black marks on their administrations.

The good thing (usually) about these two factors is that, ultimately, they are empirical. To one degree or another, they are measurable—market share gain, profits, revenue growth, territory captured, and so on. Time will tell whether your decisions were solid or misguided and whether your execution was a success or a failure. And although history can be harsh, sometimes it can also be kind. Given enough time, history may well decide that even your most crushing defeat was a noble one, and that your most glaring strategic error was a product not of your bad judgment but of the "fog of war" and other factors beyond your control.

The third, less obvious factor that will affect your legacy is *reputation*. This is what people think and will say about you—and there is almost nothing you can do about it. You may flatter, buy, or intimidate people into a polite silence for a while—but eventually, especially after you are gone, nothing will constrain them from expressing their true feelings about you. And when that historian or doctoral candidate or biographer comes around, you will pay for every moment of cruelty, indifference, or lack of empathy you had as a leader.

You can't stop this from happening—even the greatest leaders have had their detractors—but you can mitigate it. And a good way to start is by managing your entire leadership career with an eye on how the future will treat you. One way to do this is to appreciate that as a leader, especially of a large organization, most of your followers will have no more than a handful of direct encounters with you. And that is what they will remember about you, the stories they will tell others, which over time will contribute in varying degrees to your legacy.

As Joe DiMaggio famously said when asked why he played so hard even while hurt: "There is always some kid who may be seeing me for the first or last time; I owe him my best." As a leader, you should have a similar philosophy: every follower you encounter may be seeing you for the first or last time, and they will never forget that encounter. If you are having a bad day and treat them shabbily, that is your legacy to them, what they will remember and will tell their children—and historians—some day. You owe it both to them and to yourself to be the best that you can be.

Conversely, it is the subordinates whom you deal with on a regular basis who will render the most accurate judgment of your true character. Over time, they will see through any guise you put up— which is why this book argues that you must ultimately be congruent to your true character. You will be known, over time, for who you really are. Save yourself and your followers some time and energy— just be yourself from the beginning.

There's more. When your followers, as individuals, look back at their time with you or your time with them, they will be left with memories not of details about discrete actions, but instead about how they *felt* (or feel now) about working in the organization you led. Specifically, they'll reflect on the *four* things that likely created the taste left in their mouths at the end of your relationship:

1. *Reward*—Were they *acknowledged* for their commitment, and their accomplishments? Did this acknowledgment take place publicly in a forum of their peers? And were they recognized personally, by name?

It is crucial to use the power of public forums to acknowledge accomplishments, sacrifices, consistent excellence, and courage.

One big reason for this is that whatever it is you publicly acknowledge will end up becoming what people strive to achieve. So be careful what you reward with public praise. For example, don't reward heroism if the organizational culture is one of always making last-second diving catches—you will only get more of this risky, brinksmanship-type behavior. Just as you get what you inspect instead of what you expect, so too will you reap what you reward. Most people are junkies for peer acceptance and admiration. So be mindful of this—but don't let the fear of unexpected consequences keep you from rewarding superior behavior. Just do it thoughtfully.

2. *Respect*—Were they *appreciated*, privately, for their service and sacrifice? Obviously, in a public forum where accomplishment is being acknowledged, there will be the customary "thank you" moment, perhaps accompanied by a tangible reward of some kind. However, as a separate act, the power of a private thank-you— heartfelt, sincere, delivered as a separate conversation—can be even more important and more meaningful. Unfortunately, too many leaders miss this opportunity to use the positional power they possess to "bless" the actions they want to reinforce.

There are many things to thank people for, and the thank-yous that reinforce the organization's values present a double-barreled opportunity: to both let someone know personally how much you appreciate them and what they do, as well as a chance to underline and turbocharge the value they exemplified. Here are examples of thank-yous that reinforce values, either verbally, which is emotionally more satisfying, or via a handwritten note (not e-mail), which the recipient will cherish even longer:

- *Commitment:* Thank you for your commitment to customers, Sam—you really took care of XYZ (customer) in a way that makes our company look good in the eyes of the people that make our paychecks possible. I know that what you did was not easy, and it took some perseverance to stay with that problem for two weeks and nail it.

- *Courage:* Thank you Sally, for your courage in confronting that thorny issue at the meeting last week. I know you put yourself out there and took some personal risk to say what you said, and if you noticed, the whole meeting changed when you spoke up. I know how hard it must have been to do that, and I want you to know it made a huge difference, and I appreciate it.

- *Passion:* Mary, I don't have to tell you that this project has been a long, hard haul. And if it wasn't for your passion for the project—your optimism, and your endless energy—I'm not sure we would have made it this far. Thanks for keeping us all going.

- *Leadership:* Dave, thank you for stepping up and running the emergency team to fix that mess. It's situations like that that can kill an entire initiative. So it's good to know that I've got leaders like you out there willing to make that added sacrifice for the rest of us.

- *Teamwork:* Look Don, I know you're no fan of Liz. So I just wanted to let you know how much I appreciate your putting those feelings aside and working with her on the team. I know it took a lot. Thank you.

- *Dedication:* Leslie, you put in more time and energy on this project than anyone, and I wanted you to know that those long hours you gave to the company were both noticed and appreciated. And now that it's over, we intend to make it up to you for all of your sacrifices.

- *Responsiveness:* Honestly, Terry, if you hadn't spotted the problem and acted so quickly, I'm not sure we could have saved that account. At the very least it would have taken years to clear up the bad blood that would have resulted. Thanks for being there and for tackling this potential disaster without waiting for approval.

- *Independence:* Let me say it right up front—thank you, Bill, for not listening to me. That's a hard thing to say sometimes, but the simple fact is that you were right and you knew it. And it took a lot of guts to stand up to the boss and follow your own best judgment. I hope you don't make this a habit; but at the same time, I also want you to always follow your own wisdom—and I'll try to give your opinions a much more thoughtful hearing in the future.

Needless to say, that last one can be the toughest to deliver, because it requires you to recognize not only someone else's success but also your own failure. But all great leaders make it a point to identify their own mistakes and flaws (even Machiavelli counsels this!) because it not only humanizes them to their followers, but, more cynically, it gives them ownership of these weaknesses rather than letting their enemies define them.

3. *Award*—Were they *credited* appropriately for their contribution to success? Rewarding superior contribution can take several forms—money, citations, promotions, career opportunities, and new challenges. A financial reward is the award most people think of first, but it is not always the best vehicle—would you trade a college degree for the equivalent tuition money?

Money awards can also be tricky, because in practice money is much more a demotivator than a motivator. Pay too much and you look like a chump and will lose your followers' respect; pay too little and you sow resentment and ultimately lose key talent. This doesn't mean you shouldn't give monetary awards—on the contrary, there are moments when cash is crucial—but you should pay double attention to determining the sweet spot of the proper amount.

The other award forms present their own challenges. Commendations and honors are easy and cheap to bestow, but give out too many and you will cheapen their value. As for promotions and career opportunities: you have only so many to bestow, and you want to award them for what people can do, not for what they have done (remember the Peter Principle). And if you create too many ceremonial titles, you'll both cheapen the titles themselves and make the org chart top-heavy.

So what's the message in all of this? Once again, it is legacy: choose the right awards for the right occasions and the right recipients. And don't make those awards based only on the current advantages of doing so; base them also on the long-term implications of having those awards and awardees in your organization.

4. *Education*—Did they *learn* valuable things from being part of the team, or were they used by the organization with educational feedback in return? There is an optimal ratio of "give" and "get" on which most people thrive. They want to contribute to make the team a near-term success. But they also want to learn in order to improve their own long-term chances. An imbalance either way usually makes for lousy memories—and a knock on your legacy.

Here are some questions you should regularly ask yourself about your subordinates:

- Are you paying attention to the opportunities for your team members to learn by being part of your organization—both formally (classes, seminars, certification) and informally (mentorship, new challenges)?

- Are you making available professional development and training, either on-site or through scholarship programs?

- Are you offering new assignments and challenges that test and grow new skills in your people and allow them to gain valuable experience?

- When your people leave the organization, are they substantially more skilled and experienced at their craft—that is, do they have a better chance for moving up in the world from having been a part of your organization?

- Did you help them prepare for the next challenging opportunity—either with you or elsewhere—on their career path?

This can be a tough one, because it requires some generosity: you know that this training and experience you provide will also increase the risk that some people will leave you. But it is still the right thing to do, and the ones who stay will be hugely valuable. And, yes, it puts greater pressure on you to lead them well.

All You Leave Behind

It behooves you to overcome the natural tendency to dismiss the departing as enemies, fools, or unworthy and instead get to know them better and understand both their motivations and the memories they will take with them.

One of the most stunning and disheartening discoveries that psychologists have made about working people is that many employees tell the truth about themselves, their jobs, and their bosses—for the first time only during their exit interview. It is typically the first time they truly feel liberated and safe enough to state their true feelings.

That is a very sad statement about most organizations. It is also tragic—the information you need to run a better ship is there, and it doesn't emerge until someone leaves. Just imagine how much more functional and productive most enterprises would be if those same employees had been able to speak that openly while they were still there. Smart leaders are in a perpetual search for that truth, and they cultivate an organizational culture to help them find it—even when they know they might not like what they learn.

Exit interviews teach us other things as well. For example, *people join companies and they leave bosses*. I'm always amazed when this fact surprises leaders. After all, most of us have, at one time in our career, joined what was generally considered to be a good company, but eventually left because we couldn't stand our boss. The simple fact is that the organization usually is only the backdrop for our activities, but we have to deal with the presence of the boss every working hour of the day. This suggests that although it is always good for a leader to devote considerable attention to cultural issues in the organization, that focus must also be matched by the constant monitoring of the people running that culture—and the weeding out of those managers who don't fit in or, worse, who drive top talent out of the organization.

Another discovery is that most *people don't leave for a better situation elsewhere, but to escape the one they are in.* It is comforting to tell ourselves that the reason employees are leaving is because they want more money or a shorter commute or more time with their families—or that they are looking for a new or different challenge. Indeed, many exiting employees will say just that when asked, in order to meet the interviewer's expectations or avoid confrontation or because they just don't care to help their old employer anymore. But when you drill deeper, it becomes obvious that most departing employees aren't running *to* something better, but are running *from* something they can no longer bear.

What were these "unbearable" situations? And what do the *best and brightest* hope to find in their new place of employment or membership?

- *They didn't think they could make a difference*—and no one ever told them they could. They would like to be inspired and valued again—just like they were promised when they first joined.
- *They were underacknowledged and underappreciated*—they would love to have someone, especially someone "up the ladder," notice their work and let them know it matters.
- *They didn't like their boss, and their boss didn't care.* They would like to have a more respectful relationship with the person or people leading them. You may know the expression "People join companies, and they leave bosses."
- *They were treated like a helper instead of a contributor.* They would like to be given a real challenge—some meaningful work that would register on the scoreboard as part of a winning strategy.
- *They were giving too much and not getting enough*—not just financially, but in terms of learning, satisfaction, relationship,

and challenge. They would like to invest in the future of the company—and they'd appreciate a commensurate commitment to their growth.

Note that almost every one of these "unbearable" situations could likely be improved, even remedied by leadership that pays greater attention to the individual worth of employees, that recognizes and honors their accomplishments, and that supports their desire to improve themselves and become better and more productive workers. How much time would you be willing to spend each day to answer these needs and keep these at-risk employees tucked in and adding value—especially now that you know they hold your reputation in their hands?

Collective Memory

Reputation is not the specifics of one person's experience, but the broadly held collection of memories, stories, and beliefs that is the product of hundreds or thousands of points of view. These perspectives ultimately coalesce to create a publicly held and largely unchallenged opinion of a leader's mark on the world and the people of his or her time.

Although reputations quickly lose their accuracy when it comes to a specific case, they are usually more or less correct, and they certainly correlate to most people's informed view. In the business world, think of Steve Jobs or Jack Welch, Andy Grove or Larry Ellison. Over the years, the reputation of these men vacillated wildly, from genius to monster, from success to failure and back again. In a small way, this is true for everyone in a leadership position, big or small.

Eventually, however, when enough time has passed, the wide swings in reputation for all but the most famous leaders (who must forever deal with historical revisionism) eventually settle down into a single, monolithic image. In the venture capital world, we call this the "elevator pitch"—the one-sentence description of a new company that plays a surprisingly important role in whether we choose to invest in it or not. Hollywood producer Mel Brooks is a legend for selling his movie ideas in a matter of seconds. And think of the speeches of Lincoln, King, and JFK.

Leaders have their own "elevator legacy," and it typically emerges after they've retired, and certainly after they have died. Here in Silicon Valley, I can stop almost any businessperson, ask them to describe David Packard, and get in return: "Valley pioneer, founded Hewlett-Packard, legendarily enlightened business leader."

Dave Packard was a lot more than that, good and bad, but in the crucible of reputation, almost everything else has been burned away to leave only this—a reputation that one would imagine Dave would be pleased with. Notice that there is no mention of HP's products, or Packard's stint as under-secretary of defense, or his founding of the Monterey Aquarium, or the Packard Foundation, or his enormous contributions to Stanford University. One hundred years from now, should HP fail, perhaps only the "pioneer" and "enlightened business leader" descriptors will remain—but they are likely to endure.

Personal development coaches love to have their clients sit down and write their own obituaries as a way to put their lives and achievements in context. But too often this turns into a exercise in résumé writing or self-disclosure. I'm going to suggest instead that every few years you ask yourself: *If I had to pitch other people to invest in my career as a leader, and I had just a few sentences to do so, what would I say? What is my elevator legacy?*

What to Do

There is a certain sense of helplessness that goes along with every discussion about one's legacy. Too often, it seems to come down to the opinions of other people, over whom you no longer have any influence, taking place after it is too late for you to make a difference.

That's not entirely untrue. Nevertheless—and this is the point of this chapter—it is still possible to be proactive about your legacy from the very beginning of your career as a leader. It won't guarantee that the future will say good things about you; but it will certainly improve your odds.

So, what can you as a leader do *while* you are leading, real-time, to create the look-back talk that you'll be proud of?

1. Live the Nine Essential Skills

It should be pretty obvious to you by now that if you follow the precepts of Unusually Excellent leadership that we've just marched through in this book, you will have a very good chance of having an exemplary career and leaving behind a terrific legacy. After all, a celebrated leader by definition is almost always known for being trustworthy, authentic, courageous, decisive, and a empathic communicator. So if you concentrate on those things, with one eye cocked toward the ongoing state of your reputation, you can be pretty sure that your legacy will be a good one—even if you ultimately fail to reach your goals.

But there is more to a great leadership career than the Nine Essential Skills, powerful and enduring as they are. There is also one's dynamic behavior during the activities of everyday working life as a leader. Here are more of those quotidian things every leader should do.

2. Pay Attention to Change

Life is about change. Not only is change inevitable, but we *need* change. However, most change is hard. That's why there are entire shelves filled with business books about change management—so we needn't investigate the topic in depth here. What *is* crucial for you to know now is that change requires, at a minimum, a little empathy and a lot of patience. You need to be compassionate with others as they prosecute a substantial change in their circumstances—a new job, new boss, new quota, new project. These changes often throw people off for a while until they find their sea legs. Too many talented people have been lost by organizations because "they no longer fit in," when in fact they are just taking a little longer to adapt. Don't attempt to deny or resist change—just help people get through it better than they could if left to their own devices.

3. Get More Curious, and Smarter, About Human Nature

As leaders, we tend to gravitate toward the objective (facts and figures) and away from the subjective (the messy world of human behavior and motivation) because the former seems so simple and the latter so complicated.

I'm going to argue that in many real-life leadership situations, because we are dealing with people as the subject matter, just the opposite is the best path of action. Objective data often turns out to be not so objective after all, but riddled with biased data, opinion, hidden errors, false verifications, and unknowns. By comparison, for all of their perceived complexity and irrationality, most people exhibit just one of four basic emotions during important moments— and everything else is just a derivation of these four:

- *Glad*—Getting what they want when they want it
- *Mad*—Not getting what they want in the present
- *Sad*—Not having gotten what they wanted in the past
- *Scared*—Believing they won't get what they want in the future

It is as simple as that. Commit to knowledge this little matrix, which is time-tested to be true, and you will immediately find yourself looking underneath the anger, the disappointment, or the fear to find the event that caused the emotion that is currently in front of you. And if you can keep in mind that most basic states of emotion are simply a function of one's relationship with "what you want," then the first great question you need to ask your subordinates as a leader is: *What do you want?*

You won't always be able to fulfill that desire, but simply checking in, in a sincere and respectful way, can often defuse the emotion. And better yet, sometimes the answer you get will give you a simple and elementary insight into the mind of the other person—their fears, their expectations, their unmet desires, their dreams, and even the unhappy past they carry around with them that colors everything they do. Just ask. Sometimes they'll decline to reveal a glimpse into their heart. Perhaps they'll tell you more than you wanted to know, which you need to manage. But often they'll share exactly what you needed to know and exactly what they needed to say; they were just waiting for you to ask. Remember, if you don't like people, if you don't willingly embrace the whole person, appropriately, you should seek another line of work.

Related to the predictable emotional responses to getting—or not getting—what we want, it is also useful to know what reaction to expect when the information or data that we all want or need is missing. *Anxiety* is the state of not knowing what is coming but assuming it will be bad. When people say they are anxious, ask more about their fear. No one is anxious about the lotto ticket they just bought—either it can only be good, or it was just a $5 shot in the dark. However, someone could be anxious about their upcoming performance review, their son's grades due next week, or the lab report from their blood tests that they anxiously await. Learn to notice what anxiety looks like and ask the questions that allow you to know whether this is your concern—or theirs.

Excitement is the state of not knowing what is coming and assuming it will be good. When you are faced with excitement, dig for the expectation being assumed or imagined—it could be wildly out of context, and you can then head off an impending disappointment. Or it could be an appropriate response to what looks like some good news around the corner.

Curiosity is the neutral state—with no prejudgment about the possible outcome. Curiosity is mostly good, because it keeps the mind open. Foster curiosity when you locate it—it will spread like wildfire once a few influential people model the behavior. Suddenly everyone is a bit more curious, and thus a little more open minded, and that is a good problem.

Learn to work with these basic ideas, and you'll find your conversations with team members to be easier, more informative, more insightful, and—for them—more important. They will intuitively recognize that you do, in fact, want to know *how* they feel, at a basic level, and *why* they feel that way at this moment.

I'm not advocating any kind of amateur psychoanalysis—not by a long shot. What I am advocating is that a leader's currency is his or her people. People, including you and me, are complex in many ways, most of which leaders aren't formally trained to deal with. But most of us are simple and predictable in other ways, as we've just described. The human condition and thousands of years of evolution prove reliable around some basic cause-and-effect relationships, including risk and reward and working from self-interest.

Working from those basic understandings of human behavior, in conversation with your people, is a good place to start when getting to the bottom of something you wish to know or understand. The power of inquiry is difficult to overstate. When in doubt, start asking sincere questions about the things that you don't know or don't understand. If you execute these conversations with basic knowledge and care, the results are almost always positive, and people feel heard and cared for. Many times that's all they really need.

Just listen. Sometimes you'll get a freebie here—a gift—and the obvious next steps will emerge, often from the simple words that fill the void if you can bite your tongue and let someone just talk to you. Of course, you shouldn't always stay silent. But 99 percent of the time what you will hear isn't about your fixing the complaint or problem—at least at that moment—but about their being heard. Often you'll be unable or unwilling to get involved, but it is still comforting to your followers to know you care. Asking some questions and caring about the answers does not mean an implicit promise to fix anything or everything (and once you open that door, you need to tread carefully around implicit expectations), but I'm guessing it is well within your leadership capability to manage this balance between inquiry and expectation or entitlement. At the very least, and of primary importance, you will have a deeper understanding of the people who follow you, and you will have garnered an appreciation and gratitude from those who know that you cared enough to engage.

4. Give Feedback

Nobody is a perfect fit with an organization, project, or team. Everyone needs to adapt—and as leader, it is your duty to reinforce and shape their behavior to accelerate and fine-tune achievement of that fit. One of the best ways to do that is through immediate, useful, and honest feedback.

Feedback from the boss is powerful, and you always must be wary of having an impact that is disproportionate to what you meant. Still, it is the best tool you have to connect, add value, and create relationships different from the usual arm's-length management relationship. This feedback takes several forms:

Positive feedback—which reinforces things that are working well. Positive feedback from those in power blesses the work of the rank-and-file, and there is nothing sweeter to most workers on the front line than to hear words of praise from the boss.

Negative feedback—which, delivered with care, allows for course correction and improvement. Done properly, with the right intent, and with respect, negative feedback inspires most people to redouble their efforts.

Leveraged feedback—which is designed to produce new results. It is often craved by subordinates in need of guideposts in a changing strategy. If done well, it absolutely changes behavior for the better.

5. Celebrate Success

Take the time—officially endorsed and led by you—to celebrate your team's accomplishments and victories. These shouldn't be occasions to merely hand out awards and checks, but also for everyone to reflect, recharge, and feel good about what they have accomplished. And it is up to you to lead this process.

Celebrations have more importance than we usually give them credit for. For one thing, they create an institutional memory of winning, and register the accomplishment as possible. They also say "We did it." This is especially important when a "mission impossible" was successful against all odds, or a BHAG (again, that's a big hairy audacious goal) was achieved. History has shown that when something once considered impossible is accomplished, suddenly it looks easy: for example, within a year after Roger Bannister broke the "unbreakable" four-minute mile barrier, thirty-seven more people ran sub-four-minute miles. Once people realize that something is possible—and celebrations ensure that they do just that—they approach it differently and with greater confidence.

6. Respect Life Outside of Work

This is tricky ground. People have very different notions about privacy and the mixing of public and private. So, as a leader you'll find it is usually prudent not to try to know too much about your subordinates' lives beyond the basic facts. What *is* important for you to remember as a leader is that your people do have private lives outside of work, that those lives are important to them, and that, as a matter of principle, you must respect those lives.

There will be times—not many, I hope—when it becomes obvious that something is just not right in the private life of one of your people. It will pay off in the long run for you as a leader to master the skills and conversations needed to appropriately discuss this topic, to respect your people's needs, and sometimes to give the benefit of the doubt to a valuable but temporarily distracted subordinate. In the process, you build loyalty, emotional equity, and a reputation for caring about all aspects of your people that will serve you always—not just while you are in charge, in the form of increased commitment and loyalty, but when you are gone, in the form of a reputation for respecting people and their lives and families. To my mind, there is no higher praise for a leader.

OK, you are probably saying to yourself, *these precepts seem pretty obvious: respect your people, give them useful feedback, celebrate their successes, help them adapt to change. They are almost management clichés. How come so many otherwise talented, competent, serious leaders completely whiff this whole Chapter Nine topic area?*

You're right: it happens all the time. And it happens for the most avoidable of reasons:

- *You are oblivious.* You are too caught up in the day-to-day life of a leader to do any of this. You are production-minded and results-oriented—so who has time to stroke other people's egos? They are getting paid to do their job, not to whine. What's obvious doesn't communicate. Of course you have an impact on people. Duh. But you are too busy to be bothered with this right now. You have a low EQ.

- *You are afraid to engage.* Your employees aren't your friends, and you may have to fire them someday, so why get emotionally close to them? You worry that inquiring about their personal troubles is too getting too intimate. This attitude often comes from a fear that you can only safely have easy conversations with people. Thus, if you knew how to have all kinds of conversations with people, you'd be more willing to engage without fear. This is a bad reason to stay disconnected—and it is your fault, not your subordinates'. Get some training.

- *It is not a value or priority to you.* Just because you don't personally value this stuff doesn't mean it doesn't matter. In fact, it probably matters even more than it does for leaders who do make the effort, because you just may have created an emotionally dysfunctional organizational culture. Moreover, just because you don't value the feelings of others (and you should ask yourself why), those other people *do* value them. And leadership isn't about you—it's about them. These people are exactly like your customers—without them, you don't have a business. So even if you have to pretend to be a human being, treat your people like you need them—because you do.

Your Greatest Legacy

If this is the formula for leaving a great legacy, why not just follow the instructions and fake it 'til you make it? That sounds much easier than adopting all this psychoanalytical, care-about-everyone-all-the time stuff—which feels like a *lot* of work.

Go ahead. This book isn't about saving your soul, but about becoming a great leader. On the one hand, if you want to live out the Nine Essential Skills and remain internally unchanged in the process, the results can still be the same. If all goes well, most of your people, happy to find themselves in a well-run organization that recognizes their efforts, will never know that you just couldn't commit to your own growth. They will look back at you fondly—and you will deserve your good reputation.

On the other hand, unless you are a sociopath, it's hard to imagine that you will be able to consistently fake this enlightened behavior, year after year and decade after decade, without either being changed in the process or simply breaking down at some point and showing your true colors.

An infinitely better strategy is to recognize that these are the right things to do while you are leading. They produce the best results, the most productive team, and the greatest chance for success. It is only an added attribute that, in the long run, they also contribute to your reputation—and ultimately, to your legacy. As Mark King said, "I don't want people to say they loved working for me; I'd rather have them say they loved working at TaylorMade. That would be a better test and statement of my leadership legacy."

As I have already said, your greatest legacy will not be the individual items on your résumé, but the emotions felt by your subordinates about you—and the institutional culture you leave behind. "The culture" is the real answer to the question: "What was it like to work here?" And it is the quality of this culture that is the real institutional measure of your success as a leader.

Thus culture previews reputation (what people think of you) and legacy (what you leave behind). And if the values you reinforced and the culture you created lives on in institutional memory and folklore, you have been an Unusually Excellent— even great—leader.

Of course, there are other factors as well that add to or subtract from one's reputation and legacy. Along with your decisions and your communications, the more subtle actions we've explored in this chapter—things that impact relationship, quality of life, quality of work, self-esteem, growth, all the things that people live and work for—will both improve your organization and, later, define your reputation. These activities are not the same as creating teams from talent, plans from ideas, or results from action—the stuff from Part Two that leaders get measured on and paid for. But they still matter and will have a profound effect—in your ability to recruit the best and brightest; in your organization's ability to learn, adapt, and stay competitive on the world stage; in your capacity to retain top talent over extended periods; and in other ways you cannot yet even imagine.

Any leaders who think of these activities as voluntary, as a side dish to their real work, do so at their peril. This is mainline work, central to the health of the organization, regardless of the importance you place on your reputation. And even if it doesn't immediately show up on the bottom line, this is real work—and it sets the stage for so many things you will accomplish that are more direct measurements of success.

That's the beauty of having perspective, of getting out ahead of your tenure and looking back through the lens of reputation and legacy: it will enable you to do the right things today for the right results in the distant future. Happy, nurtured, acknowledged people are incredibly productive, incredibly loyal, and incredibly committed—almost maniacally so. They are worth the effort.

Your leadership touches more people than you think. You don't want that touch to be the weight of your power, but rather the hand on the shoulder or the pat on the back evidencing your leadership maturity and humility. Power gets in the way of this work, so push it aside. Once again, leadership is not about authority; it is about influence.

Another Perspective

To lead well today is to lead with a vision of and a respect for how you will be judged in time. That foresight will make you more thoughtful about the implications of even the smallest of your actions and decisions. It will force you to put yourself in the shoes of the people who follow you. And it will teach you to value everyone with whom you work—if only because they will determine your reputation and legacy. It is hard to imagine a more powerful and useful leadership tool. And that doesn't even include its most powerful application: with time and practice, it will even enable you to look inside your own heart.

The Essentials of Leadership Impact

- Stand in the future and look back on your leadership. Imagine your actions, decisions, and communications standing the test of time. You can't lead perfectly. You *can* lead with no regrets for those things that were within your control.

- What people remember is what becomes your legacy. Emotion creates memories. How people feel is important. Not the only important thing, but—really important.

- Everything you do and say, has the chance to make an impact, positively or negatively. Your positional power leverages your words and actions—be they useful or harmful.

- Acknowledge others by highlighting the ways they have reinforced values in the culture.

- Imagine the exit interviews of your best and brightest— and work to fix those things before those people leave.

- Leading *change* is a special skill. Be aware of how change affects everyone, and adjust your view and your actions accordingly. Change is a time that begs for leadership stability and clarity.

- The more you understand people—human nature—the easier you will find leading them. Emotions are reasonably predictable, and you can have a plan for dealing with much of what you will encounter.

- Above all else, just do your best. That is all you—or anyone else—can ask.

● AFTERWORD

Unusually Excellent is my commitment to those of you who have chosen to lead or who aspire to leadership in any aspect of your life. I'm grateful that you have read this book, and I'm hopeful that it helped spark an idea or two that will make you a better leader tomorrow and every day after that. I want to offer, as a final idea, a context for leadership that I hope will serve you on your growth path as a leader.

Leadership is a *mentality*. To lead others with influence and impact, you must *think* through as many issues as you can, from this point of view: as a *leader of people*. There is always a business or strategic view of a situation, and that is a useful perspective. But most of what we decide or communicate as leaders has a specific leadership consequence somewhere, at some time. Holding the *mind-set of leadership* as your perspective—when you are pressed into service as a strategist, battlefield commander, negotiator, or any other role that demands your attention on a given day—will improve the quality of your choices as assessed by those you lead. Double check to make sure you've considered every situation from the context of leadership before you finalize any decision.

Leadership is a *practice of behaviors*. The crux of leading is doing the right things, doing them well, and doing them consistently. As you saw in Part Three, behavior is the basis for both culture and reputation and is a direct reflection of our personal values, revealed over time in small acts. So, while you can learn all the complicated or esoteric theories or concepts of leadership, your impact ultimately rests on your willingness and ability to do what needs to be done, do it with skill and professionalism, and, of primary importance, do those things consistently over time, in both easy and difficult circumstances, even when you don't feel like it. You will be judged, in the end, by your actions.

Leadership is a *noble profession*. It is a mission of service to others and of achieving, through people, those things that move the world forward. To the untrained eye, leading may appear tremendously egocentric, but it is really so much more about those who have trusted you to lead them. Leaders who realize this fact early on are set up to win in a very different way than leaders who live in the illusion that it is all about them. It is a journey of learning that begins with self-awareness and continues throughout a career of discovering what it is about you that others see as authentic, trustworthy, and compelling. It is not for the faint of heart, and it is not a hobby. The finest doctors we know deeply love medicine, authentically love making people healthy, and have great respect for the people who trust them to care for their well-being. Leaders can learn much from the Hippocratic Oath.

Finally, leadership is a *passion*. It is not a "job," and it is not a career for everyone. There is no shame in declining to lead if it is not for you. Leadership is a choice. It is a deep, burning desire to engage with people and rally a community to achieve greatness. That passion is both an attribute and an asset of leaders, as it creates a virtuous cycle of hope, and belief, and results that benefits everyone involved. Leadership can be difficult, thankless, frustrating, maddening work at times. It is only the passion of leading on the field—the thrill of looking other human beings in the eyes and seeing their energy, willingness, trust, and commitment—that makes it all worthwhile, in a very quiet, private way.

I acknowledge those of you who are willing to step up and lead something, anything—at whatever place on the learning curve you are at this moment. Embrace the lessons that will be there to learn, trust in your talents and your commitment, and know that while most people will often not appreciate your efforts, nor thank you for your service, you will make a difference, and possibly a profound difference, just by your act of leading. The world needs more leaders—and better leaders—for as far as we can see. Stay in touch, good luck to you, from one leader to another.

● ACKNOWLEDGMENTS

First and foremost, I acknowledge and thank my family. To my wife, Joanna, whose boundless love and unwavering support grounds me and inspires me; and to our children, Perry, Arthur, Taylor, and Andie—you all tolerate my passions with a smile, support my countless endeavors with patience, and love me for who I am, all of which are essential to my well-being. And to our extended families—our mothers, Cathy and Joan, and our siblings, who form a wonderful, loving clan.

Second, to the team that made this book happen. Jim Levine at Levine Greenberg, who believed in the idea of this book and put his credibility behind that belief, and Susan Williams and Pamela Berkman at Jossey-Bass (Wiley), who are consummate professionals and were gracefully competent throughout the process. To Mike Malone, who assisted brilliantly with the manuscript, and Geoff Moore, who contributed the Foreword in addition to heaps of moral support. Many thanks to Bronwyn Fryer at *Harvard Business Review*, who had the foresight and courage to publish my early leadership work, twice, in *HBR*, for which I am eternally grateful. Particular thanks to all the CEOs who graciously contributed their insights, experiences, and wisdom to the stories and examples contained herein. Thanks also to the countless other leaders I met along the way who, at the end of a white-board talk or a presentation or a coaching session, encouraged me to "get this stuff into a book."

To the mentors and teachers along my path from whom I have learned so much, I say thank you for your generosity. Notably, the particularly great colleagues and coaches I've worked with in my career, all of whom have left their mark on my point of view about leadership and life—John Adler, Jeff Miller, Geoff Moore, Philip Lay, Tom McCook, Yogen Dalal, Blake McHenry, Gary Heil, Gustavo Rabin, David Kyle, Bob Kavner, Marijo Franklin, Barry Posner, and Mel Toomey. Of special note is the work of Pat Lencioni, whose books *The 5 Temptations of a CEO* and *The 5 Dysfunctions of a Team* are cornerstones of my advisory work, and without which there would be many more unsolved mysteries on the executive teams with whom I've worked.

To my clients—the nearly one hundred CEOs I've had the pleasure of working with and for over the last ten years. A few stand out as absolutely exceptional leaders and have been a special pleasure to know—Mark King, Manoj Saxena, Chris Michel, Scott Weiss, Dave DeWalt, John Kispert, and Ted Mitchell. Every student of leadership should be so lucky to work with leaders of this caliber.

To my students at the Leavey School of Business at Santa Clara University, who remind me what it means to be open-minded and thirsty for knowledge.

Finally, I am blessed to have a wonderful group of friends, who through thick and thin have shown a quality that I not only admire but treasure—loyalty. You guys will no longer be hearing about my plans to write a book—you'll now have the opportunity to buy large quantities for your holiday gift list.

Warm regards and thanks to all. Cheers!

● ABOUT THE AUTHOR

John Hamm is a venture capitalist and a leadership advisor, coach, writer, and speaker in the San Francisco Bay Area. He works with CEOs and senior leaders across the country to maximize the effectiveness of their leadership strategies and skills through personal coaching and executive team facilitation. John is also a faculty member at the Leavey School of Business, Santa Clara University. As a private investor and board member, John has a strong track record of successful technology start-ups, including Brocade (IPO June 1999), Military Advantage and Affinity Labs (acquired by Monster), Truveo (acquired by AOL Time Warner), Webify (acquired by IBM, 2006), and IronPort Systems (acquired by Cisco, 2007).

John has excelled in leadership and operating roles at several high-growth companies, including Whistle Communications, where he served for four years as president and CEO. Backed by Institutional Venture Partners (IVP) and The Mayfield Fund, Whistle became the leader in small office internet appliance products and was acquired by IBM in June 1999. Prior roles included EVP and general manager of advanced storage products, a $450 million business division at Adaptec, and executive positions at Western Digital in both the United States and Europe. John started his professional career at Hewlett-Packard.

John's writing has been published in *Business 2.0*, *Fast Company*, *BusinessWeek*, *Fortune*, *USA Today*, and the *Wall Street Journal*. His "Five Messages Leaders Must Manage" was the lead article in the May 2006 *Harvard Business Review*; "Why Entrepreneurs Don't Scale" appeared in the December 2002 *Harvard Business Review*. John can be reached at johnhamm@mac.com.

● INDEX